CONTENTS

FINANCIAL FREEDOM:	5
Introduction	9
Why Create ONE (OR MORE) Passive Income Stream/s?	13
Finding Motivation & Maintaining Momentum	17
CHAPTER ONE: Property Management & Rent to Rent as a Form of Passive Income and Financial Freedom	36
CHAPTER TWO: Benefits of Short Term Rent To Rent over Property Management	44
CHAPTER THREE: How to Find and Choose the Right Property for Your Rent to Rent	51
AirDNA Market Analysis Program	57
Local Ordinances	65
Best and Worst Cities for Rent to Rent (or Rental Arbitrage)	67
Finding Your Perfect Property	71
Landlords & Leases	84
CHAPTER FOUR: Getting Started	94
Furnishing and Staging	100
Photography	108
CHAPTER FIVE: Choosing Your Platform(s)	114
SNAPSHOT: THE NEW VRBO	120

CHAPTER SIX: Listing on Multiple Platforms	126
CHAPTER SEVEN: The ChannelS Manager Softwares	130
CHAPTER EIGHT: How to Maximize Occupancy and Profitability	152
CHAPTER NINE: BOOKING LEAD TIME & PRICING METRICS	169
SNAPSHOT: CANCELLATION POLICY	173
CHAPTER TEN: UNIQUE AIRBNB STAYS TO MAXIMIZE REVENUE	178
CHAPTER ELEVEN: Writing the Optimal Listing	189
20 QUICK TIPS TO MAKE YOU A SUPER HOST	208
CHAPTER TWELVE: Easy Automation for Passive Income	216
SNAPSHOT: CRAZY GUEST EXPERIENCES!	246
How to Stay Bed Bug Free	250
Do NOT Let This Happen (Ever)	252
CHAPTER THIRTEEN: ADditional Airbnb-Related Income Streams	255
CHAPTER FOURTEEN: RENT-TO-RICH SUCCESS STORIES!	303
CHAPTER FIFTEEN: THE TAKEAWAY	313
FINANCIAL FREEDOM : HOW TO MAKE 7 FIGURES PASSIVE INCOME WITH AIRBNB RENT TO RENT RECAP	323

FINANCIAL FREEDOM:

HOW TO MAKE 7 FIGURES PASSIVE INCOME WITH AIRBNB RENT TO RENT

The Exact and Precise Step-by-Step Formula to Create 7 Figures Passive Income and to Reach Financial Freedom with Short Term Rental, that Anyone Can Follow.

By **Fab Bale**

To my "Soul Sister" Veronika, without whom this could have never been possible.

To My Beloved Mother Eliana and to my Beloved Grandmother Gina, you'll forever be crazily missed. I love you from the bottom of my heart.

And to my Father, Peppo.

THANK YOU.

> "Real estate is like Jack and the Beanstalk's goose that lays golden eggs. It's something that pays you month after month, whether you are working or not."
>
> *-Kathy Fettke*
> *Real Wealth Network*

> "Every person who invests in well-selected real estate in a growing section of a prosperous community adopts the surest and safest method of becoming independent, for real estate is the basis of wealth."

-Theodore Roosevelt

"I don't live to work, I work to live."

-Noel Gallagher

INTRODUCTION

You may have come across this book because you read my first book, "*Passive Income : From Broke to 7 Figures in 12 Months: An aggressive 2020 Step by Step Guide to the Creation of Passive Income Streams and Financial Freedom.*"

Or maybe you've landed here because you Googled "Rent to Rent" on your laptop or you researched "How to profit from Airbnb" while you were riding the subway to work at seven o'clock this morning.

Better yet, you've talked to someone you know who has used this program to quit their job and work just a couple of hours a day **raking in a six or seven figure income** without buying any property at all, and with zero up-front investment.

Sound too good to be true? Let me tell you a story.

Don was stuck at his nine to five job. He was thirty-two years old, graduated from business school a decade ago, and had worked in project management for the same large automotive company for the last five years… but he didn't seem to be getting where he wanted to be in his career, and especially not with his income, nor was he getting what he wanted out of life. He felt incredibly stuck.

Done was (and is still) married with two small children at

the time. He was working long hours, sometimes not getting home until seven or eight o'clock at night after fighting rush hour traffic, just about time to tuck his toddler into bed, give his wife a break with the baby, warm up some leftovers for dinner, and then go over the reports to prepare himself for work the next day.

He and his family hadn't taken a vacation in years. He was exhausted and his relationships were starting to suffer. And then he had a college friend come into town on business. To his wife's chagrin, they put him up in their spare room in their finished walk-out basement for a couple of days- just during the conference and one extra day to hang out with old friends.

The last day, when his friend was about to leave, this old buddy of Dan's said something that really lodged in the back of Dan's brain... and he just couldn't shake it.

He said, "Thanks, man. Your place was so comfortable. **I'd pay to stay here** over some cookie cutter hotel any day."

It was a nice compliment... And of course, he was kidding about paying to stay in Dan's BASEMENT... or was he?

Dan's beautifully finished basement has: a nice separate entry with a small patio, one bedroom, a full bathroom with a shower (no tub), a small living room that they used for a playroom at the time. It was furnished tastefully (by Dan's stylish wife) with a couch and armchair, coffee table, and large flatscreen TV in the living room and a queen sized bed, small dresser, and smaller tv in the bedroom...

It was cozy and clean, modern and bright, perfect for one person or maybe even two.

Dan couldn't stop thinking about what his friend said, and that day at work he started looking into AirBnB. He had stayed at one once when he went to a conference in Denver, Colorado and remembered having a really good experience.

FINANCIAL FREEDOM

He talked to his wife that night. They agreed to consider it, and they did a little bit of research. After just one day of thinking and putting the numbers together, Dan and his wife set up their finished basement and listed it on AirBnB.

Since they lived close to a conference center and not too far from a big concert venue and a big outlet mall, as well as a University and some of the big automotive companies, their listing had a booking within twenty minutes of putting it online.

They priced it low and listed it as a room in the host's house. But then, after they made a bit of revenue, they decided they could make considerably more money if it was a "whole property" private suite.

They only invested a tiny bit-- two chairs for the patio, a microwave, a coffee pot and small hotel-style refrigerator, a keyless entry system, a lock for the top of the stairs going into their house, and professional photos of the space.

They priced their "private suite" at $90 per night, the average rate for BnB's in the area and less than the average hotel... and within an hour of their updated listing going live, they'd booked it for a five night stay-- a woman traveling for business.

She gave them a five star review and they were really off and running.

In that first month, Dan's basement suite brought in $1600. The next month, it brought in $2,250.

That's when Dan and his wife decided to rent a second location. They found a nice condo close to the University and convention center- a one bedroom, fully furnished with a full kitchen.

They priced it at $120 per night, a fantastic deal compared to the hotels in the area, and booked it out 25 nights that month. With their rent at $900 per month, they made roughly $2100 from that unit.

Now, between their basement suite and their one bedroom condo, Dan and his wife are making roughly $4,350 per month and Dan decided to quit his job and do this full time.

He **followed this program,** adding four more properties to to his portfolio - two in the same area and two in vacation destinations that he found through his AirDNA research (you'll learn more about AirDNA in the coming chapters), and now **Dan makes seven figures** working part time from anywhere in the world - he and his family take regular vacations and he is home for dinner every night... unless they are playing in the sparkling blue waters on their beachfront vacation in Tahiti, in which case, he's at the restaurant for dinner!

No rush hour traffic. No working through the weekend. No late-night reports to read. No more feeling like he's stuck working for someone else at a job that's not going to take him where he wants to go.

Dan owns his own business making more money than he ever could have at his old job. He's working on his own terms, and he did it without ever purchasing any property at all.

All he had to do was understand the market and rent the right places in the right locations.

With the rent-to-rent model of short-term-stay real estate, you'll be able to build a highly profitable business - yes, up to seven figures a year - without ever having to purchase property!

Your earning potential is only limited by your own drive and desire to create the kind of life you want!

With platforms like Airbnb, Vrbo, Flipkey, Booking.com and more, you can turn rental homes, condos and apartments (even yachts and yurts) into revenue into the seven figures.

Are you ready to change your life?

WHY CREATE ONE (OR MORE) PASSIVE INCOME STREAM/S?

If you're like most of us, you can identify with Dan at least a little bit. In fact, the majority of Americans dislike their jobs so much that they're actively looking for another job. A better opportunity. Something with more vacation, a shorter commute, better policies, more upward mobility.

Yes, you read that correctly-- MOST Americans do not like their jobs.

According to a recent large-scale study by the nonprofit group Mental Health America, in conjunction with the Faas Foundation, and reported in The Washington Post, **71% of Americans are so unhappy with their jobs that they want out and are actively job-searching.**

Why do so many Americans hate their jobs?

Well, there are a number of reasons Americans are unhappy in their workplace. 45% of these unhappy workers feel that they are not being compensated well for their job quality, and close to the same number think that management doesn't recognize their work or that they're overlooked for promotions.

One of the biggest and most prevalent reasons, however, is **stress.** About ⅔ of workers feel their job stress contributes to unhealthy behaviors like drinking (or abuse of prescription medications).

Think about what the effects of this kind of long-term chronic stress alone does to your physical health, your mental health, and your personal relationships.

Here's what stress does to you biochemically:

When you're experiencing stress, either the instant fight-or-flight variety or the ongoing slow-burn of chronic stress, the hypothalamus of your brain sends out the stress hormones - adrenaline and cortisol. This, of course, is good if you're being attacked by a mountain lion or your child is trapped under a rolled-over car. These hormones help give you the superhuman strength it takes, in one big rush, to help you get away or lift a one ton-vehicle off of your helpless child.

However, this kind of stress and the hormones that it releases are not good if they're produced by a nagging, daily stressors because you're getting a non-stop flow of these hormones... and that's very taxing on all of your systems.

In fact, chronic stress leads directly to a number of seemingly rampant conditions ranging from unpleasant to life-threatening, including: Insomnia, heartburn, shortness of breath, high blood sugar, headaches, weakened immune system, pounding heart, cardiovascular disease, stomach aches, leaky gut, erectile dysfunction, low fertility, menstrual interruption, muscle pain and spasms... need I go on?

Let's just say that stress is very bad for your health.

So imagine now that you're suffering from insomnia and erectile dysfunction along with a weakened immune system - so you're always sick. How does that play out in your personal relationships?

Well, not so good. Plus, the actual hormone imbalance caused by high grade chronic stress has a direct link to higher rates of depression.

Now you're sick and missing work, depressed and struggling with your relationships...

So, let me ask you a very important question. Why are you literally making yourself sick and jeopardizing your marriage, your friendships, your family, for this job that you can't stand?

I know. I get it. I'm not judging. I was there.

Many people are in that very same spot, just like Dan was at one point in his life. It's hard to take that leap into a new life where you are your own boss, doing something you love, with tons of time for your friends and family, for travel, for sleep...

I get it. Change can be scary, even if it's positive change.

But you don't have to rip off the bandaid all at once. Like Dan, and like myself, you can do it slowly, building the foundation while you still work at your nine to five... if that's what you need to do to ease into it.

OR, you can rip the bandaid right off and be making your new life right away. It's your choice.

If you read my last book, you know that there are thousands of opportunities for passive income, a myriad of businesses waiting to be purchased... but, like me and like so many countless others, you landed on rent-to-rent as your first jump into the life you want to lead.

This is fantastic! Because, in my humble opinion (and the numbers show, too), rent-to-rent is the fastest, biggest payout for a passive income stream with the revenue leaping up into the seven figures mark.

Real estate is a golden egg.

In fact, real estate is such a huge money-maker that most millionaires dabble in it on the side... if it's not already their primary source of income.

In the last two decades, 90% of the world's millionaires built their wealth through real estate investment.

I'll take it a step further to say that the world's wealthiest real estate investors are not just millionaires, their net worth is in the multi-billions:

- Lee Shau Kee - Net worth of **$28.6 Billion**
- Hui Ka Yan - Net worth of **$26.8 Billion**
- Yang Huiyan - Net worth of **$23.4 Billion** (richest woman in Asia)
- David and Simon Reuben - **$18 Billion**
- Donald Bren - **$17 Billion**

The list goes on.

How did they amass such wealth in real estate investment, you might ask? Well, the stories of these billionaire tycoons are all very different.

One inherited a property investment company from their father and enlarged it through strategic business moves, another made one good investment that rolled into the next and the next. But the point is that they all got to where they are now by different paths along the same road - real estate.

The key to good real estate investment is to get started early, and choose the right location (which we dig into in depth in Chapter Three). But, what if you don't have any money to invest?

That's where this phenomenal new rent-to-rent method becomes invaluable. You don't need to invest much *or any* of your own financial capital to get started in this business.

What you do need is the knowledge and motivation to change your life... just keep reading.

FINDING MOTIVATION & MAINTAINING MOMENTUM

When I started my freelance consulting business on Upwork and Feverr four years back, I was sitting at the beach working on my laptop (tough, right?) when I realized (not too hard to figure it out) that the place I was working from in the Canary Islands is (obviously) the perfect vacation destination. The weather is gorgeous year round, the water is sparkling, the hospitality superb… I knew then and there that I could make money on real estate in this location. Before too long, I was renting several properties and had a solid passive income stream from short-term-renting these listings.

I'm now able to work just a few hours a day, from anywhere I please (the beach in California, a coffee shop in Paris, the mountains of southern Spain) and easily afford the lifestyle I want to live.

No rush hour traffic. No boss. No suits and ties. No time clocks.

Vacation? No problem. Most of the time I'm simply working from vacation.

My life has become infinitely richer because I made that move, at that moment, from that idea that sparked while I was sitting on the beach.

But how do you get motivated to make that move, too? And then once you're invested in it, how do you stay dedicated enough to see the changes you desire through to fruition?

Motivation, by definition, is the desire and the drive you have within you to accomplish your goals.

One of the primary factors in people maintaining motivation is to set small goals that immediately yield results. Why? Because when you can check those smaller things off the list, it releases endorphins in your brain that make you feel good, happy, accomplished… and those feelings propel you forward into bigger and better goals.

Short-term rent-to-rent is an ideal business for seeing immediate results with a broad opportunity for growth.

While an investment in purchasing real estate can take years before the property value appreciates, or decades before rental income pays off your initial investment, rent-to-rent can show a profit in the very first month!

Also when you buy a property with a mortgage, always remember you are creating a broad liability. That is not an asset.

And, it's not out-of-reach for you to completely replace your annual salary in just six months following this rent-to-rent approach.

So, like Dan in the opening chapter, you can start by renting out a room in your house. Or, you can find a landlord willing to do a zero-down profit-sharing lease (more on that in Chapter Two). Once you see an immediate profit on that, you invest it back into your company and rent a second property.

Following the model laid out in this book takes a different kind of **mindset**-- this the passive-income entrepreneur mindset starting to emerge.

Unfortunately, if you've developed a different set of habits based on an active income and the product of being a slave to spending, it's going to take some time and effort to change your old behaviors.

I spelled this process out in detail in my last book, "Passive Income: From Broke to to 7 Figures in 12 Months", but it's so important to understand this concept that I want to reiterate these **seven habits of a passive-income entrepreneur for you right now.**

Here are the steps you need to take, the habits that you need to cultivate, to become a successful entrepreneur:

1. **Free yourself from excessive spending. Save to Invest and use savings as Money Leverage to increase wealth faster.** While you may be living under the assumption that freedom means buying whatever you want whenever you want, the truth precisely is the opposite. The real freedom is in the ability to say "no" to things you don't really need... or the things you don't REALLY want. When you live simply and minimally, you'd be surprised at how much money you actually have. When you stop spending frivolously, now you can use that money to invest directly back into your passive-income business. Do you see how that comes full circle? Your available wealth grows exponentially when you embrace this "no" type of mindset. Less equals more, literally.
2. **Focus on your passive income stream potential.** It's time now to be hyper-focused on your business. Ask yourself these questions: What are you good at? What assets do you already have? What are your strengths and weaknesses? What do you love to spend your time doing? Use all of the answers to these questions to formulate your business model. If

you already have a spare room in your house, that's an asset you can use for your rent-to-rent income stream. If you're a photographer, you can definitely use that! I challenge you to spend some time thinking about what you have and what you enjoy doing. Life is too short to, one, reinvent the wheel, and two, work every day doing something you don't love - let alone hate.

3. **Read (at least) one book a week.** We get so caught up in the world of social media and media in general, spending countless hours surfing through videos on Instagram or commenting on the Facebook posts of people we never met whom we call friends, playing online games and binge-watching series on Netflix, that we often forget there's a whole world of knowledge right that at our fingertips that does not require a charging dock. Books. Take a few hours out of your week and read a book. It doesn't have to be a business-related book, but of course, it could be. I learned much of what I use in my businesses now simply from reading profusely throughout my adult (and young adult) life. Read the biographies of successful people. Read self-help and motivational books. Read classics. Read the books from the New York Times bestseller list. The more, and the more varied, the better! Not only will you learn a great deal, books are a fantastic way to connect with people. You'd be surprised how people react when you can converse about a book you've both read. Which brings me to the next point.

My Recommended Book List
Never Eat Alone, Keith Ferrazzi

The Power of Habit, Charles Duhigg

Think and Grow Rich, Napoleon Hill

How Successful People Think, John C. Maxwell

Secrets of the Millionaire Mind, T. Harv Eker

Measure What Matters by John Doerr

Predictably Irrational by Dan Ariely

Founders at Work: Stories of Startups' Early Days by Jessica Livingston
Freakonomics by Steven D. Levitt
A Short History of Nearly Everything by Bill Bryson
The 7 Habits of Highly Effective People by Stephen R. Covey
The 4-Hour Work Week by Timothy Ferriss
Big Magic: Creative Living Beyond Fear by Elizabeth Gilbert
What the Most Successful People Do Before Breakfast by Laura Vanderkamp
The Gratitude Formula by May McCarthy
Steve Jobs: The Exclusive Biography
Losing my Virginity by Richard Branson
The Snowball: Warren Buffett and the Business of Life
The Facebook Effect: The Real Inside Story of Mark Zuckerberg and the World's Fastest Growing Company
Deep Work by Cal Newport
The Topeka School by Ben Lerner
Exhalation by Ted Chiang
Get Out of Your Own Way by Mark Goulston, MD and Philip Goldberg

4. **Connect with people.** Have you ever heard the saying, "Your net worth is your network?" It's time to meet more people, especially if you don't already have a broad network to rely on. Put on a clean pressed shirt and go to the next meeting of your local chamber of commerce, hit the gym, talk to the guy that's reading The Wall Street Journal at the table next to you at the Starbucks coffee shop. And I'm not

saying to push your business on them. Quite the opposite. Be interested in them on a human level. Connect with them. You never know what wisdom they may impart, or what kinds of connections they may be able to make for you. Increase your connections and increase your revenue potential - it's all related.

5. **Brainstorm.** This is all the time. Keep a pad of paper on your kitchen table or a big sheet of art paper on your wall. Jot down ideas. Do it all the time. Write down your idea, even if it seems crazy or impossible. Remember, the first person to stick a plastic lid on a coffee cup, everyone thought was crazy. Once in a while, take a look at all these crazy ideas and randomly choose one. Write that one idea at the top of a piece of paper and then write down all the ways you can make it work, and how much money you'll make as well as what kind of lifestyle benefits will come about when you do. Allow yourself to feel the excitement as if you're about to embark on this new business venture! (And maybe you even do it.)

6. **Set your goals clearly.** With a pen and a notebook, write down your specific goals for your rent-to-rent business. Keep a separate ledger for each passive income stream and write down your short-term and long-term goals for that business. Write down not only financial goals, but physical goals as well. Now, create another notebook for your personal goals. You might write down, "Take a two week trip to Tahiti" for a one year personal goal. For a one week business goal, you might write, "Book out five days on the condo." As a financial goal, you may write, "Create $12,000 in passive income revenue this month." Once you write down your goal, take a few minutes to imagine that goal clearly. How does it feel when you have accomplished that goal? It may sound silly, but close your eyes and truly try to put yourself in

the space of having achieved what you set out to achieve - and then feel the emotion of how that feels.
7. **Express gratitude.** This may sound like froo-froo, but more and more highly successful people, whether it be in athletics or real estate or the health and wellness realm, credit their regular expression of gratitude for helping them achieve their goals. Gratitude, by definition, is a deep appreciation for someone or something, and it doesn't necessitate a verbal "thank you." Gratitude is often a simple acknowledgement or understanding that someone or something helped you, or sacrificed for you, to better your life or situation. When you express or feel gratitude, it strengthens your connection to others, improves your sense of well-being, increases your level of optimism, it makes you happier and stronger and healthier (like physically healthier). Having gratitude requires you to set your ego aside and understand that you cannot, and will not, do it alone. But, you will find, with gratitude, you WILL do it and it will be easier than if you had tried to do it alone.

Now, with these seven habits taking seed and beginning to grow, you will find yourself feeling more and more motivated and in the right mindset to change your life and start working on your own terms, allowing the money to flow to you in a passive stream of income from your new rent-to-rent business.

And I'm even going to give you a bonus one, here. It's a tip or a concept that we don't often think of, but I find it goes a long way to keeping your morale up and your motivation rolling. That tip is:

Surround yourself with positive people.

I don't mean people who smile all the time and always seem

perky. We all know that those people are just plain annoying. What I mean by this is for you to surround yourself with a community of people that are supportive of your new venture, and who can see your vision or who have, in general, a positive point of view of life. Even better, surround yourself with people who are entrepreneurial-minded, who are go-getters, who aren't afraid of a challenge.

Nothing can stop you in your tracks faster than a friend or family member who says *you can't do it.* (Typically these are the people who are also unhappy in their own lives, and don't believe that they can change either.) You tend to, consciously or subconsciously, believe what you hear repeated often enough.

Nobody needs that kind of negativity... especially when you're working hard on trying to change your life for the better.

In the wellness community, one popular piece of advice to people who are trying to lose weight is to stop hanging around with people who eat unhealthy. Why? Again, psychologically speaking, water tends to find its own level.

Your friends and family, the people you see and hear every day, have a huge impact on your mindset. Make that a positive influence and see how quickly you succeed.

Surround yourself with people who consume a healthy diet of positivity, strength of character, and zest for life!

MOTIVATION CHECKLIST
✓ Stop excess spending. Increase your "save to invest money leverage"
✓ Focus on your passive income stream
✓ Read a book a week (at least)
✓ Connect with people, anywhere and everywhere
✓ Brainstorm constantly

> - ✓ Set your goals clearly
> - ✓ Express gratitude
> - ✓ Surround yourself with positive people

STOP! Do this before you go any further!

You've made it to the end of the introduction, but before you go any further, before you even look at the worksheets or the following chapters, I have to ask you a very important question:

Have you ever stayed at an Airbnb (or a Vrbo or any other short-stay vacation rental)?

If the answer is "no," the first thing I want you to do is go to Airbnb.com on your computer, or download the app on your phone, and **plan a quick trip**. Just one or two nights in an Airbnb in your very own town or city.

Find the condo on Airbnb with the highest ratings and most stellar reviews in your area. This does not necessarily mean that it will be the most expensive listing, of course. But staying at a place with a five star rating and a superhost will help you understand exactly what will make a guest in a property in your city have a top-rated experience.

Why do I want you to do this?

This is all about learning about the business, and about learning from the best.

Because if you've never experienced looking for the right Airbnb on the app (that one with a great rating that calls out to your sense of taste and style with all the perfect amenities), if you've never booked or paid for a short-stay rental property or unlocked a lock box and let yourself into someone else's home that you found on the internet…

If you've never ever been an Airbnb guest, it will be harder

(I might go as far as to say impossible) for you to understand what it is you need to do as a host.

So, having said that, here's what you do when you take your mini-vacation in your rental property: From the moment you book to the moment you leave, take note of how the experience is working out for you!

What was your general impression of the experience as compared to your typical mode of travel accommodations? Was the host responsive and friendly? Was the home/condo/apartment stylish, clean, and comfortable?

How did it feel when you walked in the door? Were you able to find it easily? What little perks made the stay feel more comfortable?

Was there anything that you didn't like about your Airbnb experience? How could it have been better?

Take notes of everything you notice about your experience... but of course, don't forget to enjoy your time away!

If you have been an Airbnb guest in the past, I encourage you to get started reading and then book yourself an Airbnb again, noticing everything through this new lens as a potential host.

The other thing you can and should do is go through the process of booking a vacation rental through the other platforms (Vrbo, Booking.Com, and Flipkey) to see how they compare. Make notes about things like ease of use, aesthetics of the online experience, and then when you take your vacation/ visit to the property, note the same kinds of things asked about the Airbnb above.

While this step isn't absolutely mandatory, it can give you a good solid sense of how the platforms compare to one another.

Nothing beats first-hand experience to give you a good feeling for what you like, what you don't like, what works, what doesn't, and ultimately what listing channels you'll choose when you decide to list your property.

EXCESS SPENDING WORKSHEET

Directions: List ten things that you could cut out of your weekly spending, along with the estimated cost and then total your weekly savings.

EXAMPLE:

Shoes/Clothing $100 / week

Costs to Cut

1. _____
   _____

2. _____
   _____

3. _____
   _____

4. _____
   _____

5. _____
   _____

6. _____
   _____

7. _____
   _____

8. _____
   _____

9. _____
   _____

10. _____
    _____

Cost saved per month = 4 x _____(total)

INCOME STREAM POTENTIAL WORKSHEET

Focus on your passive income stream potential. Answer the questions below, and reassess often. This will help you figure out the best way for you to start streaming income with minimal effort (and maximum enjoyment).

Identify your strengths. What are you good at?

Identify your weaknesses. What would you rather outsource?

What do you enjoy doing when there is nothing you have to

do?

What assets do you have or have access to (including capital)?

READING LOG

Reading a book a week (at least) helps you stay on track and expands your knowledge base in multiple ways. Remember, you can read self-help, motivational, success stories, autobiographies, and even novels. Use this log to keep track until reading becomes a habit.

WEEK ONE
Title:_____

List three main ideas or highlights from the book here:

WEEK TWO
Title:_____

List three main ideas or highlights from the book here:

WEEK THREE
Title:_____

List three main ideas or highlights from the book here:

WEEK FOUR

Title:_____

List three main ideas or highlights from the book here:

CONNECTIONS WORKSHEET

Much of building a successful business (and a happy life) is the human connection. In this worksheet, put a checkmark next to all of the places listed that you could see yourself connecting with someone. When you have made a simple connection with someone at one of those places, cross it out. My guess is you make more connections with people than you think.

- ☐ Coffee shop
- ☐ Supermarket
- ☐ Concert
- ☐ Business conference
- ☐ Workplace
- ☐ bar/club
- ☐ Chamber of Commerce event
- ☐ Church/ place of worship
- ☐ Golf course
- ☐ Gym
- ☐ Tennis Club
- ☐ Swimming pool
- ☐ Beach
- ☐ Restaurant
- ☐ Dog park
- ☐ Kids' School event
- ☐ Networking events
- ☐ Hotel lobby/ grounds
- ☐ Hairdresser/ barber
- ☐ Mechanic/ oil change
- ☐ Post office/ UPS
- ☐ Florist
- ☐ Volunteer organization
- ☐ Other _____
- ☐ Other _____
- ☐ Other _____

BRAINSTORMING WORKSHEET

This is the space to let your imagination run free. Don't judge yourself or your ideas. Put away your inner editor and just write. Use the space below to jot down any and all ideas for passive income that you could see yourself pursuing. Come back to it often, and remember to circle the ones you've pursued!

GOAL-SETTING WORKSHEET

Writing down your goals gives them a lot more weight and provides you with clarity. Goal-setting keeps you on track and keeps you motivated. In this worksheet, write down your short-term and long-term goals.

My Physical Goals

Today:
_____

This-Week:
_____
_____

This-Month:
_____

Six-Months-From-Now:
_____
_____

One-Year-From-Now:
_____
_____

Ten-Years-From-Now:
_____
_____

My Financial Goal

Week _____

Month _____

Year _____

Decade _____

GRATITUDE WORKSHEET

Gratitude is the foundation of building a successful business and leading a successful life. Keep a daily gratitude journal to help remind you of the things, big and small, you have to be thankful for. **For each thing, write "Thanks for...." 12 times.** Do this for a week and watch it become a habit and new thought pattern.

Monday, I am grateful for...

Tuesday, I am grateful for...

Wednesday, I am grateful for...

Wednesday, I am grateful for...

Thursday, I am grateful for...

Friday, I am grateful for...

Saturday, I am grateful for...

Sunday, I am grateful for...

CHAPTER ONE:
PROPERTY MANAGEMENT & RENT TO RENT AS A FORM OF PASSIVE INCOME AND FINANCIAL FREEDOM

It's long been understood that a sure-fire path to wealth is through well-placed real estate investment.

While that still absolutely holds true, the old idea of actually owning the property you're obtaining that wealth *from* is obsolete... or at least, more complicated than it used to be.

How can you possibly be a real estate investor without ever purchasing any real estate?

Welcome to Rent (Long Term) to Rent (Short Term), or "R2R", and the Financial Freedom you deserve... with no property to purchase and a work day so short, you can't even call it a day!

Before we get started, let's define some terms.

Property Management is the overseeing of real estate. In this case, it would be apartments, condos, detached houses, or even a single room in a house. In some cases, it could also be a renovated or a brand new RV (like an Airstream), a yurt, a tent, a treehouse, or a yacht.

Rent to Rent (R2R) is a legal agreement between a landlord and long term renter wherein the renter pays a fixed rent for a period of time (typically one year with option to renew) and then sublets the property on a short-term stay basis.

For the purposes of this book, we are not considering the the version of Rent To Rent wherein you rent a home, divide it out, and sublet the section to multiple *long-term* renters.

In fact, many cities and especially rent-controlled urban areas (or suburban neighborhood associations) have laws and regulations in place limiting traditional subletting because they claim it creates crowded homes that require a lot of attention, and the practice, while legal in most jurisdictions, can be dubious.

You might consider the traditional subletting route if...

Let's imagine you have the opportunity **to purchase** a six bedroom villa on the beach in Florida. It's your dream home, but you just can't quite get it on your income. You may consider some housemates, long-term renters, for a few of the extra bedrooms.

With this model, you have to be prepared to live communally, so you want to make sure you vet your potential roommates carefully. But with the right renters, you can have a really wonderful experience renting long term.

In a situation like this, you may even think about mixing the two-- sublet three of your extra rooms to long-term renters and Airbnb one or two rooms. Just make sure that your housemates understand that this is the situation when they sign their subletting agreement.

In this course, we are talking specifically about **short-term rent to rent**, which means there is one tenant in the home at a time for a short period, like a weekend or a week.

Your rental unit becomes like a bed and breakfast, a vacation rental, or more comparable to a hotel with you as the host, than it would be to a sublet long-term lease.

Passive Income is the best kind of income! Why? Because you don't have to be actively involved to bring in money, and that way you can create multiple streams of it at the same time. Passive income is the earnings derived from rental property, limited partnerships, or any enterprise wherein you're not actively involved.

This means that once it's set up, you're not really working! (Doesn't that sound good?)

Financial Freedom means that you are no longer controlled by your income. You have enough money coming in or on hand to have the lifestyle you want to have, and your choices aren't limited by lack of funds.

Financial freedom is incredibly liberating. It allows us to spend our time living lives how we want to live them, rather than living just to work and come home.

Financial freedom is the goal, and this is the strategy that's going to get you there, fast!

The "Old Way" to Manage Properties

Before we dig into the new way to operate your property management business venture, let's recap the "old way"…

The lease, the landlord, and the tenant. This is the trifecta of the traditional property management schematic.

In a traditional rental situation, an investor (let's call him Joe Money), purchases a home or a condominium with the intention of renting it out via a lease agreement.

For ease of use here, let's say that home had a sale price of $100,000. (The median home price in the United States is currently $200,000, but we are assuming Joe got a great deal in a cheaper area, he bought a small condo, or an apartment. Now, when the owner does not intend to occupy the home, the lender typically requires a minimum of 20% down on the property, so Joe Money put $20,000 down on the home and his mortgage payment is $500 per month.

He's paying off only $4800 per year because some of that mortgage payment is interest and taxes. It's going to take him 16 years to pay off that mortgage.

Now, he's the landlord, and rents the home to a renter for $900 per month plus utilities. Joe Money is making $100 per month, without repairs or any additional costs he may accrue. At this rate, Joe Money will have his initial investment of $20,000 down payment repaid after 16 years and a half.

Now, his $800 rent will all go toward repaying the remaining $80,000 on the loan. This will take over 15 years considering a 4% yearly interest mortgage at 20 years and assuming the home is fully rented the entire time.

So, all said and done, the $800 rent will become pure revenue after one and half decades of consistent rental.

Having said that... traditional real estate investment can still be quite profitable in the long run, especially if you're getting in on a location in a hot market that's about to see a rise in property value! You can see more about traditional investment in my first book, *"Passive Income : From Broke to 7 Figures in 12 Months: A Step by Step Guide to the Creation of Passive Income Streams and Financial Freedom."*

In most cases also, buying a house is the only way for most people to get a loan (mortgage in this case) from a bank. In this situation, it would make sense to buy to rent, but only if the bank mortgage is 70% or above of the total value. Your monthly income will help you pay your mortgage and guarantee an income on top.

This way you will fully own the property as well, furthermore increasing the capital gain and adding short term rental profits on top of that. But as the bank system won't allow you to buy more than one property at a time, (unless you already have an extremely high income), the rest of your capital should be invested into a Rent to Rent scheme.

Buy only if you have enough capital to cover the 20-30 remaining out of the mortgage to purchase the house. When I say "enough capital," I do not mean strictly that exact amount of 20-30% to pay upfront from your pocket, but I mean if you have at least double that amount in cash availability to keep on investing the other half into a Rent to Rent scheme.

So, with this new way to manage properties (using a rent to rent model), you're seeing a return on your investment much, much quicker with low or zero money up front. Like, I'm talking you can turn a profit after the first month. Just one month!

And then, your net income typically increases steadily as your property gains traction on the space-sharing channels.

The "New Way" to Manage Properties

With the Rent to Rent (R2R) model, you do not have to shell out a chunk of change at the front end, making this a really good investment for someone who is ambitious but does not have a lot of financial capital or have access to it. In fact, you can start generating rent to rent revenue with zero investment up front… got your interest? Keep reading.

Typically, **if you have a little bit of money** in your pocket to start your business, your startup cost is one month's rent and a security deposit (equal to one month's rent) on a new property lease. (Of course, this will vary slightly per property.) And so for a nominal investment, you have your new rent-to-rent location essentially up and running.

Here's how it works.

Let's pretend I'm going to long-term rent Joe Money's place for $1,300 per month, plus $200 utilities. I talk to him about my intent to sublet the apartment with a space-sharing platform like Airbnb, Vrbo, Booking.com, etc. He's all good with it and we sign an agreement (see Chapter 4).

I clean it up and furnish it for just a few hundred dollars, or it's in turnkey shape (if I have found a fully furnished apartment, house, or condo, that's even better). Now, this rental is going to cost me about $50 a day ($1500 / 30) with my long-term lease.

I've checked the price and occupancy rate of local home-share accommodations on AirDNA (we'll talk about it more in detail later in the book), and they're running around $120 - $150 a night with a 75% average occupancy rate.

Short term rentals bring in approximately 15-20% (and sometimes even 25% of the total property value!!) annual revenue. If my lease is $1300 per month long term, and it sublets for short-term stays at $100 - $120 per night at an 80% occupancy (24 nights/30), I'm making a profit of $1100 - $1580 per month (2,400/2,880 - 1,300), or $13,200 - $18,960 per year just from that one small property that I put zero or almost no financial investment into. Actually, this is also the calculation that you have to do when you rent a property long term to sub-let it short term. It has to make at least two times the monthly rental lease you pay. $1,300 rent - $2,600 income, $1,300 gross profit. We'll discuss further about this later on.

That is a remarkable return-time on my investment! Don't you think?

But, you may ask, are there hidden cleaning fees and taxes and insurance and incidentals hiding in there among this "zero down" business?

The fantastic thing about utilizing a space-sharing platform like Airbnb is that the cleaning fee is in addition to your daily rate - so you charge what it costs you to have a cleaning company come in. There's nothing taken off of your net profit.

Furthermore, the platform handles taxes and they cover your space with both liability and property damage insurance. They really couldn't make it easier for you.

Don't forget, in this new model, you're not typically even responsible for replacing the heater or fixing the air conditioning unit, calling the plumber or in many cases, even landscaping. What this means is that you do not bear the cost, unless it is a damage created by some sort of misbehavior of your guests, which in that case would be charged to them using the damage deposit.

Of course, your maintenance responsibilities will depend on your specific rental agreement with your landlord (and taking on some of that - while of course subcontracting it out to make it effortless on your part, can be beneficial to your bottom line - I go over this more in the next chapter). But the point is that this type of non-ownership real estate investment has a rapid high return with very little hands-on work. It's a win-win situation.

There is a caveat that, as a short-term host you may need to offer some super quick services to your guests on occasion in the case of urgent situations or emergencies... but we will cover this in more detail in a later chapter.

And the best thing is, with a little tweaking, which I'm about to show you in the following chapters, you can be nearly totally hands-off while pulling in **a seven-figure passive income** from subletting your leased properties with space-sharing platforms like Airbnb, Vrbo, Flipkey, TripAdvisor Vacation Rentals, and Booking.Com Vacation Rentals.

In this program, you're going to learn:

- The difference between Rent To Rent and Property Management

- How to: find the right properties for your R2R
- How to: deal with landlords and leases
- How to: get started with your listing
- Understanding the different channels
- How to: choose a channel manager that's right for you
- How to: tricks and tips to maximize occupancy and your revenue
- Automation tools for totally passive income
- Additional passive income that works well with Rent To Rent
- Troubleshooting you bookings (and dealing with guests)
- Rent to Rent Entrepreneur success stories
- And so much more!

It's time for you to have the life you've always wanted. The bigger question is, are you ready?

CHAPTER TWO:
BENEFITS OF SHORT TERM RENT TO RENT OVER PROPERTY MANAGEMENT

Okay, you're ready. Now, what exactly are you getting into? In this chapter we're talking about the difference between traditional property managers and Rent 2 Rent business owners, plus **how to get going with absolutely no money to invest...**

So, here we go. As you embark on this new R2R business venture, are you actually a *property manager*? The short answer is "most likely no." Or?

Here's, to start, the difference between a full time traditional property manager and what you're doing as a remote rent-to-rent manager.

Property managers are not typically only responsible for advertising, listing, and renting the properties, they also:

- Create budgets with the landlord
- Stay knowledgeable and comply with local and federal guidelines
- Collect rent and pay taxes
- Have a responsibility to Maintain the physical property

including
- General cleaning inside and outside
- Preventative maintenance like servicing air conditioners, furnaces, chimney and gutter cleaning, foundational damage, structural damage
- Repairs to property and appliances
- Construction
* Deal with emergencies

The owner of the property (the traditional landlord), if they choose to do so, pays a property manager or a management company a percentage of the rent/s in exchange for these services or some portion of these services. Hiring a property manager allows the property owner to be more hands-off in the operation of his or her rental property, making his or her properties more of a passive income (learn more about the traditional landlord passive income stream in my first book).

If you're a property manager for a long-term lease, you can be in charge of the entire operation of the rental unit for the owner. Physical property managers generally do this as a full time job, and it can be hard work.

Managing properties in this way, while it can be an excellent job, is not the kind of passive income that will typically allow you to work a couple hours a day from the beach and bring in six or seven figures. Unless you take the role and you outsource it, hiring a property manager yourself. (You'll be working for the real estate investor/landlord who could be making a six or seven figure passive income. You want to be that guy/woman, not the property manager!)

ZERO INVESTMENT PROFIT-SHARE RENT-TO-RENT MODEL

There is another approach that lies between being a traditional property manager and a short-term-stay host. This approach allows you to start earning rent-to-rent income right away without any investment at all.

This works well with a rental that the landlord is having a hard time getting a long-term renter for at the rate they want to get from their property. With this model, you offer to sign a long-term lease with the landlord for the property (typically one or two years), without an up-front payment of any kind, which is normally comprised of first month's rent, last month's rent, and a security deposit.

Sounds risky for the landlord, why would he want to do this? Because he/she gets something in return.

In exchange, you agree to take on property maintenance and you give the landlord a percentage of your short-term rental profits every month - an amount that would exceed the amount the landlord would have charged for a long-term renter. You indeed typically earn less out of these schemes compared to Rent to Rent because of that, but you also invest nothing in it and potentially you can add unlimited property in no-time.

To more fully automate this model, you would then turn around and sign an agreement with a local handyman to make himself/herself available for building maintenance issues on a per-incident basis. That way, you're hands-off with any repairs and you still come out way ahead!

This is a win-win situation for both the landlord and for you!

Rent To Rent property management business ownership is a completely different approach than a traditional onsite property manager altogether.

As an R2R purveyor, you are acting as a "kind of middleman" between the landlord and the subletter. Depending on your agreement with your landlord, you may take on some property management components such as light ordinary maintenance, but your position is not typically as time-consuming and extensive as that of a traditional property manager.

And, you do not WORK for the landlord. You are **your own boss with your own business**.

In fact, for total automation, you may *hire* **a property manager** to handle the needs of your subletting tenants (Airbnb, Vrbo users, etc) and the property for that usage, and we'll get to that in detail in Chapter Seven.

But with R2R, your heaviest workload is in the beginning, and even that requires only a few hours-- depending on whether you're renting out a room in your current residence, renting a furnished apartment, home or condo, or if you're acquiring a new property to use as your space-sharing rental.

If you're renting out a room in your residence, you'll need to have a conversation with your landlord and perhaps sign some paperwork if he/she agrees to allow you to rent to short-stay guests. Then, you'll choose which platform(s) to use for your listing (covered in Chapter Five). Once you've made your selections, you'll fill out the host profile section as completely as possible using a good, clear headshot of yourself and nice quality professional (as possible) photos of the space.

The last step: Start renting!

For a new property, you'll need to figure out which type of property to rent and where, plus sign a new lease and perhaps furnish the space (if it doesn't come furnished) before moving on to the steps above. This process is all covered in great detail in Chapters 3 and 4.

Overall, it can take as little as a couple of days to get your business up and running! Once you're making a profit with that first rental (likely within a month), you can start using your revenue to start adding additional listings and doubling, tripling, quadrupling your income.

At this point, the "management" of your business should still only require a couple of hours a day to check in with all of your rentals' platforms, systems, and management streams - that is, if you've set it all up according to your plan.

The benefits of Rent to Rent over property management are, from a theoretical point of view, clear. You have a much smaller time commitment with a much larger potential for profit early in the game. You are essentially your own boss, running your company from your computer-- from anywhere in the world (that has internet access).

When we go further and deeper into details though, in both cases you anyway need to care operationally about the maintenance of the properties, to give your guests the highest service and the offer them the properties in best shape possible.

Maintenance is one of the key aspects of the Airbnb Rent to Rent scheme, either if you follow the property management or the R2R typical form of real estate business. As your properties need to be always in awesome condition, you cannot wait for the usual slow timing of the landlords.

Your guests will be staying only a few days, and they expect to check in into a flawless house and to have interventions within a few hours to fix anything which might be needing assistance: Water pipings, bathrooms, electricity, wifi, appliances, et cetera. They won't tolerate any delay, and that will later badly reflect into their reviews about their stay at your estate. You have to be on top of your game with it.

The only main difference is who will pay the maintenance bills at the end. In the case of Rent to Rent, only the extraordinary maintenance will be at landlord expense, while the ordinary interventions will be at tennant (your) expense.

Within the Property Management scheme instead, both will be at the landlord's charge.

How about utility bills? In an R2R, they are the responsibility of the tennant, and Property Management they are the landlord's duty.

The other main difference between the two types of rental schemes is the potential earnings. In a rent to rent scheme, the average potential earning is +100/200% of the monthly rent (for instance, total monthly rent $2,000, gross profit $2,000/$4,000). Within the Property Management type, the earnings are usually much lower. The most part of them go to the owner.

Although this depends upon your specific agreement with the landlord, usually owners are not willing to give a too high stake of the profits. Roughly around 20% of the monthly net income.

You need to be a very good dealer to be able to get a higher share, as a 20% on the gross profits or a 30/35% on net income, maybe offering a series of additional services like gardening, pool cleaning, check in-out and guests assistance, in-day urgent maintenance intervention and so on. Which means, if the typical monthly short term rental income gross is $4,000 per property, your profit will be between $600 to $1,200 each.

But do not forget, no investment upfront in this case! And no additional bills during the contract period. So we can say that roughly, rent to rent scheme will give you from 200% to 300% higher income than property management, but will also give you an initial investment (although a pretty small one) to face.

Ideal is to mix the two, adding as much property as possible when you first step into this, with the property management scheme, while investing the profits coming from it into the

Rent to Rent form. And with 40/50 listings total, you will be able to then reach the 7 figures on a yearly base.

> **SNAPSHOT**
>
> According to AirbnB's latest market report, just 1% of the Airbnb hosts generate 19% of the revenue. These hosts are the motivated men and women who have moved beyond "renting out the extra place in their house when they're not home" and into the financially-driven multi-property business of space-sharing. Over 75 of these elite hosts have an annual revenue of at least $1 MILLION. And you are about to learn the very same tools they use to build and maintain their businesses in just hours a day, from anywhere in the world. You can be part of the 1%. What are you waiting for?

CHAPTER THREE:
HOW TO FIND AND CHOOSE THE RIGHT PROPERTY FOR YOUR RENT TO RENT

Now, you've made a decision to become an R2R business-owner. Congratulations, making that decision is the first giant leap into your new life. So, you've either already started by renting out your own apartment and it's going well and you want to add a second location, or you're starting right out with a new location.

The question is, "How do I find the right property to maximize profit?"

Rules # 1, 2 and 3 are location, location and location!

This goes for all real estate investments, not just in short-term rent-to-rent. But in this business where you start making a profit right away, the impact of where you choose to rent is seen almost instantly.

In real estate, it's all about location. Period.

Now you have to be wondering, if you don't already know, what exactly does a good location mean? Here are some tips on how to look for the best location for real estate investment (particularly for short-stay rental income) that will allow you to maximize revenue in both the short and the long term.

How to Find the Optimal Location for Your Property

You're going to hear me talk about location a lot, and that's because it's one of the most important factors in your rental's success.

If you look at the statistics, and it is also just common sense, the **most successful rental properties are located near a city's attractions,** including: Historical buildings, museums, theme parks, the city centre, large conference centers, the beach or seaside, main shopping districts, transportation hubs, and/or lifts for the mountain locations.

But beyond this, you should consider some other additional factors when pinpointing your perfect rental location.

Consider Urban Sprawl

The thing about cities is that they're not homogeneous. You can't say that getting a home in the suburbs of Chicago is the same as getting one right downtown near the pier. Or that a house even a few blocks away on the South Side of Chicago is the same as getting one in the city right by the hospital. In New York, would you consider Manhattan the same as Brooklyn or Queens? You have to take a look at the city dynamically, and even look at how growth and land availability is affecting the neighborhoods and the home values in the area.

Urban sprawl is what occurs when people begin to move out of a city, and it usually occurs as a result of population growth. When people start moving out of a city as a result of population growth, it tends to be the outlying areas that suffer the most severe declines in property value, rather than in the urban areas.

Urban sprawl can also occur if a large industry goes under. The people whose jobs this industry affected are out of work and people can no longer afford their homes. In direct contrast to the urban sprawl caused by population growth, urban sprawl caused by a failing industry will cause the home values in the city and urban area to decline. This is because more and more homes and small businesses end up abandoned, foreclosures skyrocket, and neighborhoods start to deteriorate.

Take a look at the pattern of urban sprawl in the city you're considering. Are there areas of abandoned houses, rundown neighborhoods, unkept streets and closed businesses, et cetera? Or do you see a rejuvenation happening, with homes getting remodeled and park areas restored, like the gentrification of Brooklyn that started in the 1970's?

How's the Neighborhood?

Which brings us to... the neighborhood, which is important whether there's been urban sprawl in recent years or not.

While your choice in neighborhood will likely have more to do with your own personality, there are a few key factors that play into a really good neighborhood that are consistent across the boards: **accessibility, appearance, and amenities.**

As far as accessibility, what that means is that you need to see if the neighborhood is easy to get into from main routes. The drive to and from an airport, train or bus station and its proximity to city centers or attractions is also part of the neighborhood's accessibility.

Now that we've determined that we can easily get into and out of our neighborhood, we can move on to appearance. In this case, looks matter.

Are there mature trees in the area? How do the neighbors keep up their landscaping and the exterior of their homes? Are there green community spaces like parks nearby? How are the condition of the roads and sidewalks? Well-kept public areas are a big plus about a neighborhood, and poorly kept public areas can really detract for a neighborhood's appeal and value.

Also look for amenities like shops, restaurants, and grocery stores. In the case of a vacation rental, it's best if those things are within walking distance for ease of your guest's use without having to get a Lyft or Uber.

And the last thing to consider about the neighborhood is, "Is it safe?"

You can access the area's crime rates easily through Zillow or a quick Google search, and you must check them. You can also get a sense of the neighborhood's safety by driving or walking around the neighborhood. Are there kids out riding bikes, joggers, neighbors talking on the sidewalk? The presence of people enjoying outdoor activity is a good indicator of a safe neighborhood.

Future Development

Making a winning investment in property and housing, even when you're renting, can mean getting a location that's on the upswing. This means that you get in at the low end of the housing prices and see the benefit as the value rises.

So, what is coming up in the future of your property and the surrounding neighborhood? Are there any plans for new schools or libraries, public transportation, commercial property, restaurants, new homes or apartments, or even attractions? The question that's answered here is, "Is the neighborhood growing?"

If it is, that means the property values are increasing.

If you can see signs of a neighborhood that's waking up… get in on your investment now! The property you buy or rent in an up-and-coming neighborhood is only going to increase in value and bookability! That means a higher revenue potential for your listing!

Lot/ Rental Location

Now, look at where within the boundaries of the neighborhood is the actual property you're considering? Here are a few things you need to keep in mind:

While you want the house to be in decent proximity to major routes, you don't want your house right on top of the highway or the train tracks. Nor do you want it to be right smack next to the bus station. The noise of the traffic and train will be a huge deterrent to guests, and that will cut into your revenue in the long run. .

What you do want your house to within walking distance of, are: a grocery or small market, cafes, restaurants, local attractions, parks, bodies of water, and even churches.

But here's the kicker... you don't want the property to be too close (a few meters) to a church or some of these locations. Why? Because overflow parking from large churches or busy restaurants and attractions, as well as traffic from schools, noise into the middle of the night from bars or concert venues, could actually spoil a positive guest experience.

On the other end of the spectrum, a home nestled on the beach with a gorgeous view, or with a cabin with acreage in the woods on a river, will only appreciate in value... even if you can't walk to a market or a bar.

Finding the right location is all about finding that perfect balance.

Home Aesthetics

Now, let's get to the home, condo, or apartment itself. We are talking about size, space, purely aesthetics, now.

For a vacation rental, the lot size typically doesn't play a huge role in a guest's decision to stay at your property... especially if we are talking about a city location. It plays a role, just a lesser role than if someone is looking to buy property or sign a long-term lease. With short-term stays, guests are going to be looking more for a place that is aesthetically pleasing, so it's typically not as much about having a big yard as it is about having a place that's the right size and architecturally and stylistically pleasing.

Now, if you don't want to put much money upfront to get your business going (or none at all), choose a property that has a really nice curb appeal to begin with. You don't want to spend a lot of time and money putting in repairs, such as painting, updating windows, doing landscaping, fixing broken fencing (the list goes on)... especially on a home you don't own.

Here's the short list of what to look for in your property, aesthetically: paint, brick or siding that is a pleasing color and not peeling or broken; nice sized porches and clean driveways free of cracks and weeds; and newer (if possible) good quality windows. In a condo, make sure the lobby is nice and clean and the exterior of the building and any amenities visible and/or accessible to the guest are well maintained.

Now, you know what you're looking for in a rental property, and this perfect estate might be in your own backyard...

If you're already renting and it's successful, it might make sense to open a second R2R property in your own area.

But if you're not already renting, or if you're neighborhood doesn't seem like a viable option for any of the reasons listed above (or any other reason), there are some really simple, yet most professional and much more precise ways to figure out where to sign a lease for your R2R to maximize occupancy and profit.

AIRDNA MARKET ANALYSIS PROGRAM

AIRDNA is one of the best tools, if not THE best tool on the market for researching locations and for analyzing the profitability of a specific rental once you narrow down your search.

This tool can also be used long-term as you run your listing and increase your business with new properties, as it has tools to fluctuate the list price to accomodate for market value, and so much more.

This is what you'll see when you go to the AirDNA landing page.

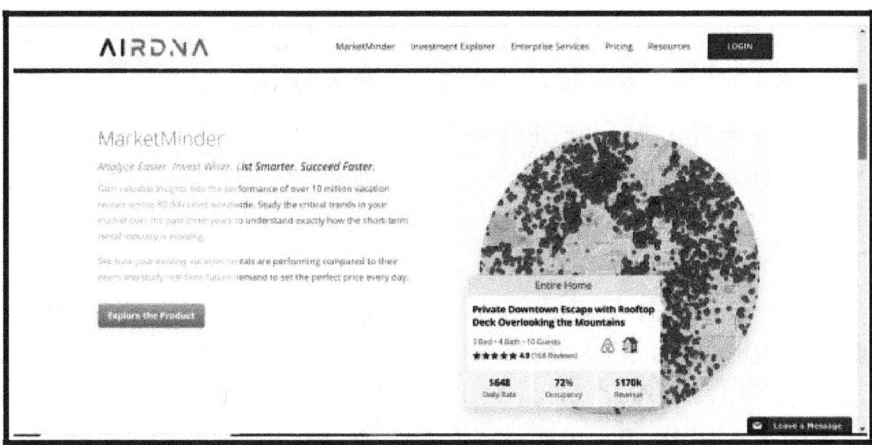

AirDNA has a number of products in their suite that are invaluable to the start and the operations of your Airbnb/Vrbo business.

Their **MarketMinder** product will help you gain valuable insight into the market trends in areas all over the world, including the average rate, occupancy, and revenue for the type of home you're considering.

There are several different options of AirDNA to choose from: The Free Account, the Monthly Subscription, and the Enterprise Account.

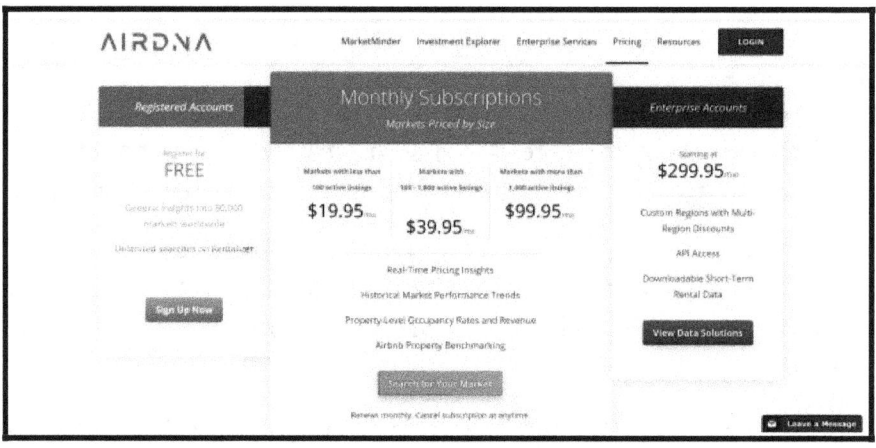

The Free Account gives you a lot of good insight to get you started with your first, or even first few, properties.

When you open up your free version of MarketMinder, you'll be prompted to enter a city, neighborhood, or zip code. For this purpose, I entered Santa Monica, California, USA. (See below.)

You can then click through the page to view different variables for the rental area. The purple, blue and green icons on the right demonstrate different types of properties, and the map allows you to zoom in on specific areas.

FINANCIAL FREEDOM

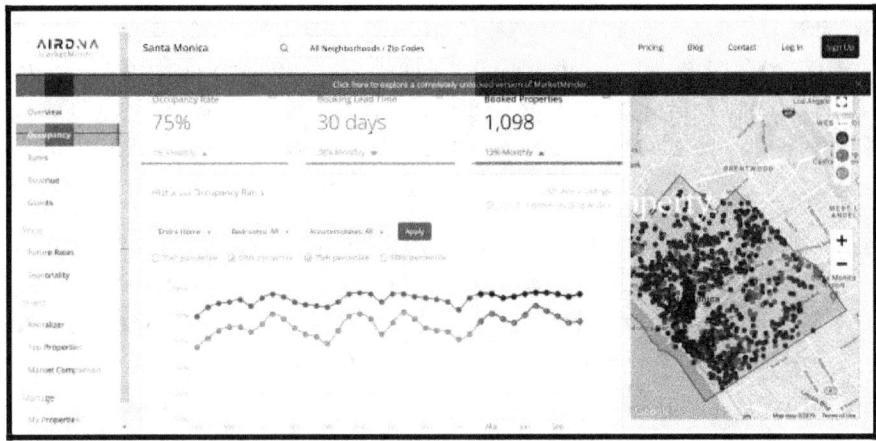

This FREE tool is absolutely adequate to get you started on your R2R business venture. It gives you information about the occupancy rate in the area and the monthly average income per single property. If the average is 75% like in Santa Monica, it means you can really top that up with a 85/90% occupancy rate (like the best properties there do) following the indications I will provide to you inside this book.

As you acquire more locations, you may want to consider upgrading to one of the paid subscriptions in order to access more sophisticated marketing and management tools. In any case, this is an extraordinary tool which I recommend taking advantage of in all its potential from the beginning.

The **Monthly Subscription Priced By Size** is a step up from the free version and gives you access to:

- Real-time pricing insights, allowing you to make immediate decisions based on the most up-to-date data
- Historical market performance trends
- Property-level occupancy rates and revenue
- Airbnb property benchmarking

The Full Version: If you have multiple listings or you're looking to grow your R2R business to have dozens of properties all across the US generating potentially **a million dollars in revenue** per annum (or even just half of it...) you should consider upgrading to the full version ($499.95 per month), which will allow you to choose where to better invest inside the entire country or across the globe. The full version will give you:

- A more detailed market analysis so that you can really pinpoint the locations with the most profitability
- Full API (Application Program Interface) allows you to more easily integrate your software for simple sharing, publishing data, and communication across channels.
- The custom regions allows you to pinpoint your specific target area to refine your search and your data

At close to $500 per month, this may not be a program you want to start with. But when you're **generating over $80,000 per month in R2R income**, a few hundred dollars a month is a small price to pay for a tool that will help you keep on top of your market value and growth potential.

Beyond the market analysis tool, as you grow your Airbnb business, you'll be able to utilize the other aspects of the AirDNA application.

AIRDNA'S FREE VACATION RENTAL CALCULATOR

The application's free vacation rental calculator analyzes over 10 million vacation rental properties listed on Airbnb and Vrbo globally and can use this data to accurately predict your rental property's short-stay earning potential. This is an invaluable tool once you narrow down your search to exact locations.

To use the tool, you simply type in the street address, click on the number of bathrooms and bedrooms and the number of people the space accommodates, and the calculator will give you your estimated annual revenue, your estimated daily rate, and estimated occupancy.

With the upgraded version of the application, you can then

pull up all of the rental properties in the area for comparison, including their listings, photos, reviews, and statistics.

With the unlocked features you can also pull up a market comparison report including annual revenue growth.

If you click on the "Overview" tab for your property, you can see clear graphs and marked maps of the rental properties in your area by channel, their rental size, growth, amenities, Airbnb ratings, rental activity, cancellation policy, and minimum stay. Essentially, you're getting a clear and complete picture of the market in your area, which will help you set competitive rates for your market area.

This unlocked feature will also show you a projected calendar of seasonality and an example of how to best set your future rates.

AIRDNA INVESTMENT EXPLORER FEATURE

With the investment explorer feature of the application, you can simply and easily localize your market strategy using market seasonality and ten other property signals.

Here is an example of an analysis of the Nashville, Tennessee market.

Nashville, Tennessee

Rentals Analyzed:	**859**
Occupancy Rate:	**63.7%**
Average Daily Rate:	**$333**

	Percentile		
	50th	75th	90th
Revenue Potential:	$48,409	$69,308	$119,246
Gross Profit:	$23,753	$44,653	$94,591

Home Value Index:	$405,500
Yearly Mortgage Cost:	$24,655 (30yr., 4.5%)

Price Per Sq. Ft:	**$341**	5yr. Change	**10.1%**
YoY Change:	**2.2%**	% from Peak:	**0.0%**

AIRDNA TOURISM BOARD FEATURE

This feature allows you to work closely with your tourism board and/or local government to advocate for the acceptance of short-term rentals as a viable and profitable means of economic development.

These features come in handy when you are trying to set up a rental unit in an area that has either dubious regulations on rent-to-rent or you are trying to change the regulations in your neighborhood, municipality, or in your condo unit or homeowner's association to allow rent-to-rent or home-sharing. Having said that, more and more municipalities and associations are seeing the benefits of having short-stay rentals, and so it's rare that you will have to put effort into changing regulations. It is, in any case, never worthy to do that. Always better to choose an easier neighborhood or municipality.

The application generates trend reports, which tracks the supply and demand rate of properties listed on Airbnb and Vrbo. This application accurately measures all critical metrics for use in interrogating your home-sharing market.

[Table: AirDNA trend reports showing Occupancy Rate, Average Daily Rate (USD), RevPAR, Supply (Nights), Demand (Nights), and Revenue (USD) for Last Twelve Months September 2018 vs Last Twelve Months September 2017, with monthly columns Oct through Sep and rows for 2017, 2018, and % Chg.]

These reports are complete and ready to present, making your presentations and executive dashboards a snap.

With this feature you can also gain insight into your market, how compression events might affect rates and reservations, and forecast your revenue and tax revenue.

The "Guest Origin Reports" section of this feature lets you understand travelers and better taylor to your target market. You can find out where your guests are traveling from, what languages they speak, and where they're finding their travel information - through which social media platforms, et cetera.

AIRDNA RESOURCES SECTION

Through their "Resources" tab, AirDNA provides a large body of resources for you to do your own research about markets, trends, and other topics relating to your vacation rental business.

This includes articles in a number of different languages, including French and Japanese, and around a lot of different topics. Some of the articles include:

- A 2019 Forbes article titled "The Rise of Vacation Rentals: Short-term Tenants, Long-Term Profits"
- "Mexico Vacation Rentals: Emerging Markets to Watch"
- EU AirDNA Index November 2019: Inaugural Report
- The Best Cities for Airbnb: Compare Markets Side by Side
- 当Airbnb房东是怎样一种体验？
- "What does the Rise of Airbnb Mean for Vienna's Property Market"

And so many more. This section is constantly being updated with market reports, press releases, How-to's, new regulations, new trends, and more. All of this is information that you can easily access when developing and increasing your short-term rental business, and I highly recommend reading these articles as they are published so that you can keep in tune with the industry as it evolves.

Again, if you're just starting out with your first R2R property, you don't need the paid version of this software yet. If you have a fully booked property, and you know adding that two bedroom house down the street is going to generate revenue, because it offers similar characteristics of yours in a profitable market, go ahead and do it. You don't need software for that.

But when you move into a bigger ballpark, shooting to obtain properties to the tune of a seven figure income, you should or even MUST consider AirDNA to assist you in your market research and in setting your prices so that you remain viable in your market area to maximize your return on investment and profitability.

LOCAL ORDINANCES

If you're using AirDNA to choose a market area, the saturation of space-share short term rentals (AirDNA uses both Airbnb and Vrbo data) will indicate the acceptance of short-term rentals in the area.

But if you have chosen not to utilize the program (clearly not my advice though, by the way) let's say you're renting that little studio just a block from the park that you saw for rent when you walked your dog... Before even calling that landlord, you should prepare yourself by knowing the local ordinances about short-term subletting.

The good news is that most lease agreements include a standard term for subletting, and that's across most jurisdictions. But there are some exceptions to that rule. So, before you sign, make sure you know you can short-term sublet that property legally.

This information is typically found easily on the city's website. For example, if you go to the NYC.gov website and type "short term sublet" into the search engine, you'll find the information you're looking for (shown below).

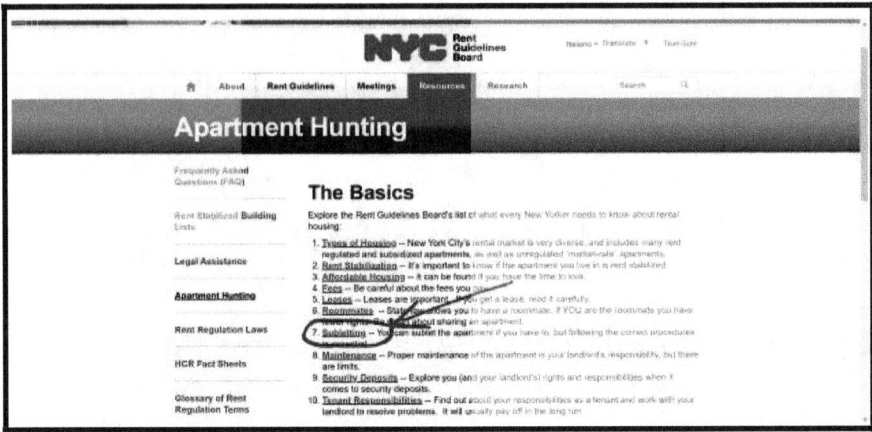

If the city's government web site is tricky to navigate or not giving you a clear answer, simply call your city offices and ask for the department of housing. They will be able to either answer your question or direct you to the correct source for information online.

BEST AND WORST CITIES FOR RENT TO RENT (OR RENTAL ARBITRAGE)

Rental Arbitrage is the actual word for what you're doing here-- renting low and re-renting high to multiple renters through a short-stay rental platform like Airbnb or Vrbo, et cetera.

And the fantastic news is that AirDNA utilized rental price data trends gathered by a platform called Zumper to pull together a list of the best and worst cities for doing just this.

To do this, they analyzed data over twelve months to find an average, accounting for seasonality. And then they took that number for both long-term rental cost and average Airbnb or HomeAway rental income, and subtracted it to determine the average for potential revenue for a rental arbitrage in the given city.

RevPAR is a hotel industry term which means "revenue per available room." This number will tell you how much you can expect to make on average per room in a particular location.

Here's what the AirDNA numbers look like for the best and worst cities in the world for rental arbitrage, divided into one and two bedroom properties:

Worst Markets for 1-Bedroom Properties *AirDNA Report

Market	Monthly Rent	Short-Term RevPAR	Arbitrage Potential
San Francisco, CA	$3,700	$3,245	-$455
San Jose, CA	$2,850	$2,108	-$412
New York, NY	$2,850	$2,548	-$302
Oakland, CA	$2,270	$1,975	-$295
Laredo, TX	$830	$545	-$285

Worst Markets for 2-Bedroom Properties

Market	Monthly Rent	Short-Term RevPAR	Arbitrage Potential
Scottsdale, AZ	$2,080	$1,677	-$403
Irving, TX	$1,490	$1,091	-$399
Chandler, AZ	$1,440	$1,177	-$263
Laredo, TX	$940	$710	-$230
Oakland, CA	$2,720	$2,631	-$89

For some of these markets, the long-term rental rate is low but the short-term rates are not high enough to make a solid revenue. In others, like San Francisco, the long-term rent is really high but you can rent out more than one room in your property very easily! This is why San Francisco didn't make the "Worst Market" list for two bedroom.

So, even if your city lands on one of those lists, it can benefit you to keep digging into the value of that market. If, however, your property is in one of the cities below, you're in a really good position for rental arbitrage.

Best Markets for 1-Bedroom Properties

Market	Monthly Rent	Short-Term RevPAR	Arbitrage Potential
Honolulu, HI	$1,700	$3,446	$1,746
Nashville, TN	$1,380	$3,043	$1,663
Boston, MA	$2,400	$3,920	$1,520
Detroit, MI	$610	$1,883	$1,273
Des Moines, IA	$810	$2,000	$1,190

Best Markets for 2-Bedroom Properties

Market	Monthly Rent	Short-Term RevPAR	Arbitrage Potential
Boston, MA	$2,750	$5,338	$2,588
Honolulu, HI	$2,230	$4,772	$2,542

Nashville, TN	$1,390	$3,580	$2,190
Corpus Christi, TX	$1,070	$2,690	$1,620
Detroit, MI	$690	$2,165	$1,475

While places like Honolulu, Hawaii might not be surprising… Detroit, Michigan? Des Moines, Iowa? Yes, indeed. These cities have really good arbitrage potential because they have year-round steady short-term stay rental traffic, perhaps from business travelers or event locations, with low monthly rent.

Now, on to the specifics of finding your perfect property!

FINDING YOUR PERFECT PROPERTY

Now that you've pinpointed your area, it's time to find that perfect house, condo, or apartment!

If you have a ZERO budget, the first option that a lot of hosts do is to rent a room in your own home, or rent out your entire home! Obviously, no need to mention that renting out your entire home only works if you have someplace else to stay for free while you do so.

Or the other option you could choose, is to manage someone else's entire estate.

I know a woman, Sarah P., who rented out her own apartment for a couple of months to get her startup money. Her boyfriend lived just a few miles away, and so did her mother. She had a nice loft in a trendy part of the city. She listed it on Airbnb and on the days it was booked, she stayed either with her boyfriend or her mother.

It did so well, and made so much money, that she ended up renting a new apartment and moving. She followed this program as well, adding four more properties and making over $120,000 per year--- as a second income! Which means, to get your 7 figures with Airbnb Rent to Rent scheme, you approximately will need 35/50 properties, and believe me, you can fully automate the entire process to keep it always as a passive form of income stream.

Sarah never quit her regular job. She is an artist and loves it, but becoming a rent-to-rent business owner gives her the flexibility to work on her commissioned art pieces with the security of a solid income.

Now, let's break down the startup if you are **RENTING your first property to list** on Airbnb, Flipkey, or another site like Vrbo.

In this case scenario, this is your first property and it is not a space in your own personal residence. You need a house, condo, or apartment!

The first step in this process is to determine how much capital you have up front to invest, and then figure out your target property based on what value that amount can bring you in the area you're looking at. This is your startup budget.

Let's say you have $2,000 to invest up front. You will want to look for a rental that is approximately $750 per month.

$750 first mo. rent + $750 security + $500 furnishing & hospitality = $2,000

This budget works well if you have a little bit of furniture already available to get you started, or if you're looking for a furnished unit. If you have to start completely from scratch, you'll likely need an additional $300-$500 for furnishings.

Now, where do you start looking?

There are a number of resources for finding homes and apartments for lease, which we will go over these next pages. But before we do, I want to recommend that as you look for your property, you stay away from any homes listed with a property management company! The best way to get a landlord to sublet for short-term rental is by talking directly to the person making those decisions.

So, try to look for rent-by-owner properties. This way you're skipping the property manager and going directly to the landlord/owner.

Remember, this is the step you take after you've already determined the best general location using AirDNA.

It's important to mention here that the online AirDNA method to discover which neighborhood is the best, plus long rental portals (described within the next paragraphs) to find the proper condo inside that specific city/neighborhood, is by far the best one, and the only one which can really guarantee you to make excellent profits if you follow my method described within this book.

Although, we should take into consideration the situation of someone who does not want to move too far from his or her own neighborhood and would like to start something close to home, also to be able to optimise time and costs.

Anyway, if you really want to make very good money with the Airbnb Rent to Rent scheme, you should seriously consider moving there where the profitability is the highest.

But If you're set on renting a property close to home, there are a number of methods to utilize for scouting locations.

The Dog Walk Method

I know it sounds crazy for me to even mention you to walk your dog to choose a property within the rental hot-spot area, and well but hang in with me here for just a minute...

One of those is taking your dog for a walk around the various neighborhoods and look for "For Rent" signs!

And if you don't have a dog, that's fine, too. You don't need a dog to go for a walk. Just put on your tennis shoes and enjoy the weather.

I know it sounds pretty silly, but you can get a great idea for the neighborhood and the property by walking around, talking to neighbors out raking their lawns, and experiencing the area in person.

Now, you've found a property that looks promising with a "For Rent" sign in front. At this point, you can either go right up to the door and knock to inquire (which can often yield great results), or you can take down the information from the sign (take a quick pic on your smartphone) and call when you return home.

Zillow Search

Zillow is a great tool for finding rental properties in specific markets.

Zillow has a database of over 110 million homes, including homes for sale, homes not yet on the market, and rental properties. This application will give you market value and other statistics as well as photos of the property, amenities, and price.

Either download the app on your smartphone or tablet, or use the website on your laptop or PC. Make sure to create a free account so that you can save your favorites and other information.

You can see here, I typed in Detroit, Michigan and filtered by "rental." You can get your listings by property or display the properties on a map of the area..

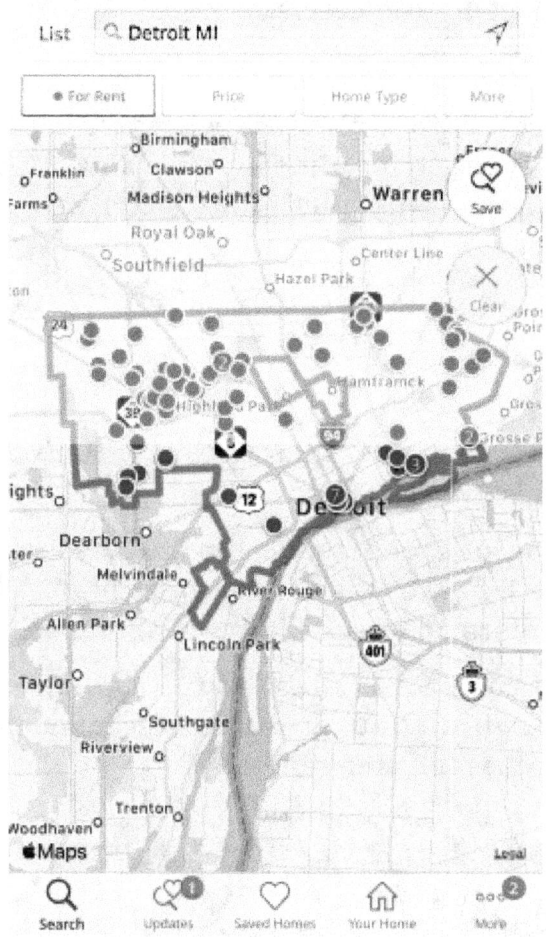

Also, through Zillow's automated system, you can click on a property, look through the photo album, ask questions, book a tour of the property, and also quickly and easily contact the landlord for more information.

TIP: I highly recommend opening up the conversation with the landlord about short term subletting once you've met with them, not on the Zillow chat application, as some landlords are not as receptive as they could be and a personal conversation or a letter (which I explain in detail in the next

> chapter) can be much more effective.

Zillow is the easiest way to explore properties without leaving your home (or even getting out of your pajamas). The application provides accurate detailed information with simple follow-up channels.

DISCLAIMER: Zillow only includes U.S. locations. This will NOT be a tool used for international rentals.

Trulia

Trulia is another application similar to Zillow. *And also like Zillow, it only covers locations within the U.S. market.*

But if you're looking for a property within the U.S., Trulia is a great place to start. It has very good functionality and a lot of the same kinds of information and filters as its competitor.

Below is the landing page for Trulia's desktop app. It's simple, clean, and easy to navigate. You can create an account and log in to save your searches and preferences.

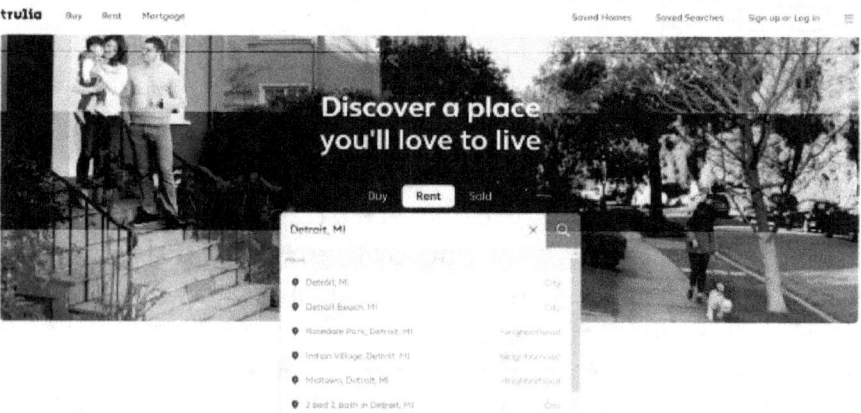

Here's what the Zillow desktop site looks like when you type "Detroit, MI" in the rental property search bar. It is similar to Zillow, but adds a nice touch with the "Search by Neighborhood" option wherein you can explore various areas within your search parameters.

This is a really nice feature that can tell you a little bit more about the area in which the listing is located, including safety reports, night life, grocery shopping, schools, parks, restaurants, walkability, and input from neighbors. It's created partly through market research and partly through input from neighborhood residents and previous short-stay guests.

You can also refine your search by price, number of bedrooms, type of property, pet allowance, et cetera. This is a standard feature to most rental property search engines.

Another fun feature of this app is that you can flip to the satellite view of the map and then zoom in on a particular area! You can see the topography, landscaping, if there are a lot of cars parked on the streets, what the major intersections look like, and more.

The application is user-friendly and has great functionality on both desktop and smartphone or tablet.

DISCLAIMER: Trulia does not include international listings. It's a U.S. only application.

Craigslist

Craigslist is one of the options that DOES offer international listings!

Craigslist is an all-inclusive classified site, similar to the classified pages in your local newspaper, only it is conveniently online! You can search for everything from a job to a bicycle to

FINANCIAL FREEDOM

pet hamster to a house, all arranged in neat categories.

While Craigslist may seem a little outdated and a bit more jumbled than the beautifully polished and taylored housing apps, it actually can be a good source for rental information.

This is what you see when you type in your location on Craigslist. (For this purpose, I typed in Detroit, MI, continuing with that theme.)

As you can see here, it's nothing fancy, but it gets the job done. Now, you can click on the "apts/housing" tab to find rental properties in the covered area.

For this search I switched to the UK, just to demonstrate the international capability of the Craigslist platform. Below you see what pops up when I clicked on "flats/housing for rent" on the London, UK Craigslist.

There were **180 listings** for "housing for rent in London, UK" on the day that I typed in those search terms.

The next task is to filter through the results. The sidebar does offer some filter options by geographic range, price, type of property and availability. However, **you cannot filter out short term rentals** from the guaranteed leases.

This means, you have to go through them all individually. Having said that, you can start your process by eliminating the listings that have such a low rate, it's obvious the given rate is for one night and not one month.

For example, if a two bedroom flat with full amenities in a popular location is listed at €50, you can assume that's a nightly rate. You can eliminate that as a contender.

Or, if you prefer, you can filter out by price to eliminate the short-term rentals. Just set your bottom price at a number that is higher than the short-stay rentals in the area (a number easily found in your AirDNA research).

Finally, click on your chosen listing and peruse the photos and property description.

FINANCIAL FREEDOM

Keep in mind, unlike Zillow and Trulia, Craigslist does not specify which amenities must be listed, so it's up to the landlord to give you complete information in their description.

Some descriptions could literally just say, "Two bedrooms." Not a great listing, but you never know what you could find out with some digging.

Finally, contact the landlord via the specified phone number, email, or Craigslist reponse.

LANDLORDS & LEASES

The next and often most daunting step of the rental process is approaching the landlord about a short-term sublet contract.

But don't worry, it doesn't have to be difficult if you put a few things in place first!

> **3 QUICK TIPS FOR WINNING OVER A LANDLORD**
> 1. Come prepared with information about the benefits TO THEM of short-term subletting and with detailed information taken from Airdna. Make a beautiful presentation, and bring out all the charm.
> 2. Offer them a slightly higher rent or a small percentage of the profit in addition to the lease agreement.
> 3. Offer to take care of minor maintenance and upkeep.

The Benefits of R2R for Landlords: Landlord Letter

When you approach the landlord about renting his or her property with the intention of subletting through a space-sharing platform, the number one most important thing to do is to make sure they understand that doing so would be valuable to them.

How do you do this in a streamlined, organized way?

I recommend a form letter with some variation of the following information. Or, consider this food for thought.

Potential Landlord Subletting Letter

Dear Joe Money,

I am interested in renting your property at 123 Main Street, but I don't want to live there! Instead, I would like to invite guests who are visiting the area for vacations, conferences, or events to stay at the house for a day or two or a week at a time.

The guests will find the home through a platform called [insert your chosen platform]. This platform hosts millions of travelers across the globe and has a proven record in excellent business practices.

Why would you want to lease your home to me? Because home-sharing is a better deal for you than leasing to a full-time tenant! Here's why.

Guests take better care of your home. *Guests of a home* don't typically do any of the annoying and expensive things that a tenant might do, like:

- Leave trash cans out by the curb for a week
- Store a bunch of broken bicycles in the backyard
- Have dogs out barking all night disturbing the neighbors
- Have cats that destroy the carpet
- Mess with or break the heating/cooling system
- Paint rooms awful colors
- Install a satellite dish on the roof
- Park too many cars on the street or in the drive
- Have problems with neighbors
- Wear out or break an appliance (guests rarely use them)

Plus, instead of having tenants whose housekeeping tendencies could be dubious, you'll have me hiring a professional cleaning service on a regular basis and keeping the premise as beautiful as possible for the next guest.

I will guarantee your rent to be paid on time every month and will handle any minor maintenance issues that may arise. Your property will be kept in spectacular condition because the better we keep your apartment, the more reservations we will get and the more profit we will make. That is just pure logic. The platform also covers [x amount] of coverage for any damage that may be caused to the property above the security deposit. So, rest assured, your home will be well taken care of.

I am excited about talking to you further!

Sincerely,

[Your Name and Phone #]

Keep in mind that the landlord of this new property may not be familiar with Airbnb, Vrbo, Flipkey or any other space-sharing platforms. They likely think of subletting as sectioning off rooms in a house and filling the it with extra tenants. You can assure them that this is not the case, and you could even offer to show them your platform and your profile on your chosen space-sharing app so they can see exactly what you mean.

Once landlords hear the advantages of renting to you, most will agree to allow subletting of their property. But, some don't. Do not get discouraged!

Sweetening the Pot

If the landlord still needs a little more convincing, offer to pay a slightly higher guaranteed rent or offer a small percentage of the property's R2R revenue (such as 2 - 5% depending on the rental value), or simply just offer a higher fixed monthly amount. Don't go too high though, and always do your homework with AirDNA. You should know in advance how much that apartment, villa, condo or townhouse could make, and how much you can pay for it. Try always to choose properties which can potentially make at least +100% of the monthly rental cost. And always try to find some which could make even +200%.

I have 10% of my houses which can perform +300/+400%. Yes, this is not a mistake. These types of properties do really exist...

The other perk you could offer is to take care of light upkeep on the property that the landlord would typically have to do him/herself. This might include things like clearing snow, replacing water filters, repairing a leaky faucet, et cetera. Of course, keep in mind that you're likely going to hire a property manager to attend to all of these duties and you will adjust your space-share fee accordingly.

By now, Joe Money is ready to hand you his keys! But hold on, there's some paperwork you need to do!

Using a Letting Agent

An easy way to find a lease property is by going through a letting agent. A letting agent facilitates agreements between tenants and landlords and is typically responsible for finding tenants, collecting rent, and other property management duties.

Letting agents already put a lot of effort into compiling a database of landlords, so why not let their work work for you?

The only problem is that you may have to spend a little bit of time and energy convincing them that renting to you is going to save them work and still give them their payout. This means you have to build a rapport with them.

Explain to them how renting to you will keep a solid tenant in their building, they will get to keep their fee, and you'll take over a lot of their management work.

Less work for the same pay-- this is a compelling argument. When you put it that way, they're likely to pitch your proposal to their landlords.

Leases and Rental Agreements

Before you can even think about posting your new property online, you must make sure you have all the proper paperwork in order, or you could end up booking out a house that you never end up taking possession of. And that would give you a really bad reputation- and a horrible host rating (we will get to why that's important in a later chapter)!

Now, what paperwork do you actually need? A lease... or a rental agreement? What's the difference? And do you need to specify that you will be subletting?

Some landlords may be super casual and want to rent on a handshake and a conversation. But the landlord-tenant relationship is complicated and regulated by a lot of laws on the federal, state, and local levels.

So, while that conversation could possibly hold up in court, it's so much safer to have everything in writing. Why?

Avoid Ugly Disputes

Legal disputes over anything from late rent, repairs, security deposits, et cetera are not only a headache, they disrupt your revenue stream. You want to avoid these at all costs.

FINANCIAL FREEDOM

What if your landlord said it was okay to sublet with space-sharing platforms, and then sees how much money you're making and decides to kick you out with the reason that "he never said that you could sublet." Now, he's just taken your business and all he has to do is set up his own profile -- after all the hard work you did. Or he/she could try to raise your rent, or ask you to perform duties that weren't agreed upon.

If you have all of the minutiae in writing, you won't have to go to court to get it resolved.

Keeping it Legal

Some jurisdictions require long-term rental arrangements (12+ months) to be recorded in writing, and some state laws require landlords to disclose certain information to tenants prior to occupancy. This is just one tiny reason why it's important to have all lease agreements in writing and filed where you have immediate access to them.

Security Deposit

Your rental agreement or lease should specify the specific usage of your security deposit. For example, if you put $1,000 security deposit down and you damage the carpet at a cost of $500 repair, you want to make sure that the balance of that deposit is returned to you after you vacate the premises. You also want to make sure that your security deposit would be used to cover any unpaid rent, and that it would be returned upon satisfactory termination of the lease with no financial or property issues. These types of things would be spelled out in the agreement.

Lease vs. Rental Agreement for R2R Property

A rental agreement establishes a tenancy for a short period of time, usually one month, and it's automatically renewed at the end of the month unless either party gives proper notice of termination.

A rental agreement gives the landlord a lot of flexibility to increase the rent or change any other factors in your agreement on very short notice (except where rent control ordinances apply).

This makes a rental agreement a poor choice for use in operating an R2R business for which you may be booking out the property months in advance. This kind of agreement is weighted toward the landlord, and is only really good for a tenant who may not wish to be bound to a long-term lease.

A lease, on the other hand, is typically a longer duration (typically one year) during which time the terms of the contract cannot be altered without express and written consent of the tenant and the landlord.

At the end of the lease term, the agreement can be renegotiated and the terms tweaked or the lease can be terminated.

The lease agreement is the best choice for your purposes. It provides you with the stability you need to run your business and it also secures a guaranteed rent for your landlord, so it's a win-win!

Your landlord may hand you a rental agreement or a lease that they already have prepared. It's important that you look over the agreement very carefully, and even hire a lawyer to do so if you're not comfortable doing it yourself, and do not hesitate to ask for reasonable changes or additions. This is your business, after all!

Here are some **key terms** to look for or add to your lease agreement:

Names of tenant(s) and landlord. This seems fairly obvious, but you'd be surprised how many legal documents have left off important and simple information such as full legal names. So, make sure your full legal name as well as the full legal name of the landlord are clearly written in the document. If you are starting this business with any partners, or there is anyone else legally responsible for the rent, also list their full legal name in the agreement (and have them sign it). This way, if there should be an issue, they are also held responsible for the payment of the contract.

This is also where you want to **make sure there are no clauses against subletting** in the lease agreement. If you want to be doubly sure, you can add a clause here specifying your landlord's permission to sublet the property.

Term of Tenancy. Note the start date, length of tenancy, and expiration date as well as the specifications for renewal options.

Property Description. This includes the property address (including unit number) as well as any storage areas or parking areas and any areas that are not to be accessible by the tenant.

Deposits and Fees. Be specific about the amount of the security deposit and its intended, acceptable, and unacceptable use. (For example, the deposit can be used to cover property damages but not to cover last month's rent.) Make sure the amount of the security deposit is in compliance with the deposit limit laws in the property's jurisdiction. Finally, specify how and when the unused security deposit will be returned after lease termination.

Rent. Include the exact amount as well as when and how the rent will be paid. It's in your best interest as an R2R business operator to have the rent automatically withdrawn from your bank account. This way, your business is as automated as possible (and your rent is never late).

Maintenance/Repairs. It's important for both you and your landlord to make the repair and maintenance responsibilities clear. Make sure any restrictions and responsibilities are clearly defined.

For example, if you (as the tenant) are responsible for snow and leaf removal, that should be specified. And if you are prohibited from painting walls or replacing appliances, that should also be specified. This way you can easily avoid any conflicts that may arise.

Property Entry. The lease agreement should clearly delineate the landlord's rights and restrictions to property entry.

Your landlord may wish to include other rules and regulations that are important to him or her, such as:

- **No illegal activity** (such as drug sale or usage)
- **No smoking.** If your landlord chooses to ban smoking, her or she may include all forms of smoking including marijuana and vaping. Or they may restrict smoking to certain areas. You should accept these guidelines and simply make them a part of your space-sharing rules. Or, you may choose to enforce even more restrictive guidelines than laid out by the lease.
- **No pets/ pet restrictions.** Your landlord may not allow pets or may restrict certain types of pets. Or, they may allow dogs, for example, but not large breeds. Make sure you know your landlord's policy and if pets are allowed, understand any rules regarding them. Again, you may restrict pets for your subletters even if your landlord allows them.
- **Vehicle limits.** Your lease may restrict the number of vehicles allowed to be parked on the property. If this is the case, make sure your subletters follow those same rules.
- **Noise restrictions**. Especially if your property is an apartment or attached condo, there may be noise ordinances included in the agreement.

If there is a policy outlined in the lease that you have strong feelings about, it's crucial to bring that up with the landlord before signing any documents. Never go against the landlord's policies, and never assume you can "get away with it." Breaking the terms of the lease could get you evicted. And trust me, the landlord will find out about it.

Contact information. Make sure that your contact information as well as the landlord's contact information is complete and accurate. If there are certain pathways for communication that are preferred, that should also be spelled out in the lease. For example, if requests for property repairs are to be submitted in writing, that should be specified in the lease agreement. Do not leave out any details.

Disclosure. In some jurisdictions, there are laws that could require your landlord to disclose information about the property. These disclosures could include the presence of lead-based paint, for example, or other potentially hazardous construction or even insect infestation history. It's important just to make sure that the agreement is in line with the local, state, and federal laws in regard to disclosure.

I know this sounds like a lot of information and perhaps a bit of a headache. But, most landlords have a tried-and-true lease agreement already in place that may simply require a little tweaking or an addendum to include your ability to sublet.

Also, you can easily outsource this by hiring an attorney to look through the lease agreement and make sure it all works! The important thing is that you get a clear lease agreement in place now, it will save you headaches later!

CHAPTER FOUR:
GETTING STARTED

How To Maximize Your Property's Potential

Okay, now you've created a great relationship with your landlord, you've got your lease signed and you're ready to list on Airbnb, Vrbo, or another platform so you can start earning money on your rental property!

Well... almost.

If you've ever scanned through Airbnb, Booking.com, Vrbo, TripAdvisor or any other kind of property listing sight, you understand how important it is to show a beautiful space to potential guests.

Let me ask you a question. These are photos from actual space-share listings. Which property would you be more likely to click on?

PLUS Entire loft · 2 beds

FINANCIAL FREEDOM

YOUR PHOTOS ARE YOUR ADVERTISING!

So, don't just go snap some flip-phone photos of a bare living room with a folded-out futon and a box tv. **You have to stage your property.**

And that means starting by **making smart choices with furnishings, housewares and decorations**. With a new unit, you'll likely have to start from scratch, which can be the most labor-intensive part of getting your business going (but also one of the most important). Your place needs to be modern, fresh and, especially, warm. Your guests need to feel "AT HOME…" That's why they're choosing a home-share over a hotel.

It's lwork to decorate your space unless you're lucky enough to have rented a nicely decorated and fully furnished property. In that case, your staging will be very minor. But for these purposes, let's say your unit is **not furnished** (like most of the properties for rent in the US).

Here are some tips to get you on the road to the best possible listing, the most beautiful photos... and the most comfortable stay for your guests, which as you know is the most important part.

And then, after you set the stage, make sure you're taking professional quality photographs of your property (do NOT skimp on that step). This can be outsourced or you can use a few simple tips to take professional-looking photos with your smartphone (keep reading - this shouldn't be your first option). My advice in any and every case, is absolutely to hire a professional. A professional photographer can make the difference not only with the shoot itself, but (especially) with the post editing as well.

FURNISHING AND STAGING

When you're considering the decorating style for your rental unit, the least expensive and most attractive choice is to go for a clean, modern, simple but warm look with perhaps one standout piece or a few inexpensive conversation pieces.

And of course, the first thing you have to consider is your budget.

Do you even have a budget? Let's say you have absolutely no money to spend on furnishing this unit. Don't worry, all is not lost!

Remember that network you built by connecting with people in your community - at the coffee shop, at church, at the beach and the networking groups? You know how you've also surrounded yourself with positive, supportive friends and family? Now's the time to reach out to your network.

And this is not a time that I recommend using a form letter or a group email, and definitely not a blanket Facebook post. A personal phone call goes a long, long way when you're asking for something for free. Free, you say? Yes.

Think about the people you know, who they are, what they do for a living, what they have in their lives that could help you... What might they have that would be useful to you that you don't think they'd mind giving up.

Imagine a call like this.

> "Hi, Aunt Sandy! How are you doing? Well, you know how I'm starting that new Airbnb business? I was wondering if you'd help me out. I know you have that blue floral couch in your basement and the last time we were there you mentioned you never used it. It would be perfect for the condo that I'm trying to furnish on a shoestring. Would you be willing to pass it on to me if I come and move it?"

Nine times out of ten, Aunt Sandy is more than happy to get rid of that "ugly" couch (which is actually vintage and perfect for your quirky loft condo). And if she's resisting, ask her to loan it to you for a couple of months until you can buy a new couch for the space.

Or what about a call like this one?

> "Hey, John! I know how amazing you are at building websites. The one you built for your daughter's music business is totally awesome. I was hoping maybe you could help me out with a simple website for my vacation rental. I will totally give you and your wife a free night for a little staycation as a thank-you!"

If John loves building websites, he would be glad to share his passion with you - especially if you've been hyping up your plan with your friends and family. And the cool thing is you can follow this same process for almost everything you need. Does cousin Chuck own a small appliance store? Maybe he can give you a coffee pot with a tiny dent in it. Did your friend Cindy just get divorced? She'll totally give you the sets of sheets from her master bedroom- she never wants to see them again. Grandma has a whole set of silverware because she's downsizing into a condo. You get the picture!

And if you can't get something you need for that first rental property, ask yourself if you really need it in your own house.

Are you willing to give up your own microwave for a month until you build enough revenue to reinvest in your property?

If so, put your own microwave in your rental unit. Do you really need silverware place settings for sixteen, two sets of bedding for your bed, twelve bath towels? Taking an assessment of your own belongings can really go a long way to furnishing your rental.

Now, maybe you do have a nice budget to furnish your new property! You have $1000 to spend on making this place feel like home. You can do this very easily with a little bit of creativity. Let's break it down.

Bedroom: The bed is the most important furnishing in this room. It has to be comfortable, or guests will not give you a good rating. So, spend the most on the bed, especially the mattress.

You can find a nice, inexpensive bed frame gently used on a number of different platforms, such as Facebook Marketplace, Craigslist, Letgo, the local classifieds, Freecycle, vintage and consignment shops, and even garage sales.

For my "Detroit, MI listing" example, I was able to find a really nice wood bed frame with head and footboard on Facebook Marketplace for $50 along with a nightstand for $10, a bedside table lamp for $15, and a small dresser for $25.

I went to the Ikea website (there is a location near the listing) and found a nice new mattress for $200. I also found bedding for $15 per set at Target, and a comforter on clearance for $45 as well as nice, fluffy pillows for $4 each. You can hit the local thrift shops for artwork and perhaps a mirror over the dresser. So, here's my rundown for my example bedroom.

Queen bed with frame and mattress: $250

Nightstand, lamp, and dresser: $50

Bedding and pillows: $110

Artwork, mirror, curtains and rods: $60

Total bedroom: $470

It's important to keep your color schemes simple and light. If it's too cluttered or busy, it could turn off potential guests - and too much clutter is a nightmare for the cleaning crew.

Livingroom: You absolutely want to have a comfortable and nice-looking couch in your living room-- but that doesn't mean it has to cost you a fortune!

An older or vintage couch in a bold color can really be an attractive centerpiece to a room. Try the same channels as you used for the bedroom for the couch (Facebook Marketplace, Craigslist, Letgo, even Freecycle). And then don't forget the tried and true brick and mortar thrift shops like Salvation Army and Goodwill.

If you find a fabric couch, make sure to vacuum it well and even consider using an upholstery cleaner to make sure it's in fantastic shape.

Much of the wood furniture and even the washable accessories like pillows and blankets can be purchased for very little expense at thrift stores!

You definitely want to purchase a television, as this is a comfort most guests have come to expect unless you're renting out a remote cabin or a retreat-type property. A Smart TV is a good option because you can allow your guests to log into their own Netflix, Amazon Prime, Disney Plus, et cetera without having to purchase a subscription or an additional device (like a Roku). Or you can add a subscription to a streaming service for a nominal monthly cost.

Couch: $100

Coffee table: $20

Side Chair: $30

TV stand: $40

55" second hand Smart TV (Ebay): $280

Throw pillows, blankets & accessories: $20

Living Room Total: $490

Bathroom: The bathroom should be simple to complete for very little money. You can find towels, washcloths, and bath mats at big box stores for $2 - $3 each.

FINANCIAL FREEDOM

Keep your bathroom bright, airy, clean and simple. This makes a good impression on guests, photographs well, and a simple uncluttered bathroom is much easier for your cleaning service to maintain.

6 bath towels: $24

2 hand towels: $6

5 washcloths: $5

Bath mat: $5

Bathroom total: $40

Kitchen: For a one bedroom unit with a small kitchen, you only need to supply place settings for four as well as glasses, coffee mugs, and silverware. If your unit is equipped with a stove and oven, you should also supply at least one pot, one pan, a baking sheet, and cooking tools like spoons, knives, and spatulas.

Also very important to the appeal of a rental space is a coffee pot or coffee pod machine.

These things can all be purchased inexpensively at most big retail outlets like Target, Walmart, Ikea, Menards, et cetera. You can also order many of these items on Amazon and have them shipped directly to you.

But, since all of these items can easily be washed well, you can get a lot for your money in the kitchen department by shopping at thrift shops.

Small table and two chairs: $25

Coffee pot: $5

Microwave: $15

Dishes, silverware, glasses, mugs: $20

Pots, pans, utensils: $15

Kitchen total: $80

Total Furnishing Cost: $1080

This may sound like a lot to pull together, but it really only takes one or two days of shopping and moving things in. If you have no eye for design, you live further away from your property, or you have no time to furnish and stage... keep reading to the end of this chapter. With a little bit more capital to invest up front, you can have this entire process outsourced completely. You never have to even go in the door of your property.

Now onto the staging portion of the decorating job.

Staging is more than just putting furniture and dishes in a space. It's about invoking a feeling. It's about setting someone down in the middle of a story they want to read about themselves.

In the age of social media, images are everything.

Staging goes beyond furnishing. Staging is about putting on the finishing touches that keep that potential guest engaged after the first click. So, you need to start by thinking about your niche.

Is your place quirky, artsy, peaceful, cozy? Does it appeal primarily to family retreats, business people, college students, sports enthusiasts? Play to your property's strengths when choosing your accessories.

If it is a more corporate feel, or if you're situated close to a convention center or business hub, consider a well-stocked desk complete with paper, pens, outlets for phones and laptops, and even an inexpensive air printer with paper.

Is it an art feel? Place a nice art-centered coffee table book or two on the coffee table and a guide to local galleries.

Is it family focused? Add a high chair or booster chair and a stack of games or coloring books and crayons on a shelf.

Is it a serene retreat in the woods with a big open floor plan? How about including some candles, a yoga mat, binoculars for birdwatching.

The draw of travelers to space-sharing over hotels is that the Airbnb, the Vrbo, they have a **personal touch that makes you feel more at home**, inspired, at peace, or more comfortable.

These items might cost you a little more up front, but they'll pay for themselves dozens of times over in increased and repeat booking.

Now that you've added your unique touches, it's time to take some photos.

PHOTOGRAPHY

You can have the most perfectly designed and nicely staged space, but if your photography is poor, you won't get clicks on your listing. And here's the thing...

Clicks = bookings = revenue!

While hiring a professional photographer would be the easiest route, and as I mentioned before, in my opinion the best choice in terms of renting / profit / occupancy results, you can take your own photos to save money at first, without any particularly special equipment or training. Please just do not forget, though, to have a proper professional photo shoot taken once you make the first bucks. That is the best investment you can make to boost your profits exponentially. But until then, here are some tips on taking your own listing photographs like a pro.

First, before you even take the first shot, walk through your house as if you were a potential guest. What do you see? What are you looking for?

Clear away any clutter and make sure everything is sparkling clean. Fluff pillows, straighten rugs, wipe windows.

Now for the actual photography:

- **Take Photos Everywhere!** Guests want to get a feeling for your home and the surrounding area. So take photos outside from the street, of the front porch or balcony, the entry, and of course all the rooms. If there's a great little strip in walking distance with restaurants and cafes, or a

beach, or a park, you should take a photo of that, too! Try to show any angle at his best, though.
- **Stage Your Space.** You've already done a nice job of furnishing your space, now make it look inviting. In the kitchen, set out coffee mugs and a treat from a local bakery or confectionery or a bottle of wine and two glasses. Put fresh flowers in a vase on the kitchen island. Light a fire in the fireplace. However your home would invite guests or make someone feel "right at home," set it up before you start photographing.
- **Time it Right!** You want bright sunlight for your interior shots rather than the yellow of sunset or the artificial yellow of electric lights. If you look at the photos above, the clear, bright photos are much more inviting.
- **Showcase Unique Features.** Does your property have something cool and interesting? Maybe you have a fire pit or a sauna, a clawfoot tub or a nice reading nook. Even consider accessibility features like handrails, ramps, or zero entry showers. These can make all the difference for some travelers. Make sure you showcase those things that would catch the eye of a potential guest.
- **Use a Higher Resolution.** Make sure you're shooting in at least 1024 x 683 pixels, but i recommend not to go lower than 3840 x 2160 pixels, or in any case shoot at the highest resolution possible. People might be pulling up these photos on a computer, not only on mobile phones, and you don't want them to look grainy or blurry. A large format, crisp photo is definitely more appealing!
- **Use Landscape Orientation.** Static vertical photos can be good for some parts of your listing, but try to avoid them as much as you can, because the search mode all turns up in landscape. So, if your photos are in portrait, they won't display properly. Portrait mode can be used for shooting some details, which will look artistic and come across well displayed in the listing.
- **Utilize your Phone's Features (or your camera's if you**

have one). Your phone likely has different modes to shoot in. Make sure you're shooting in plain photo mode with the flash turned off. Utilize your phone's light adjustment feature as well to get the best possible lighting.

- **Show Off Your Style!** Do you have a really cool Mid Century Modern couch, hand-made quilts on the four-poster beds, or some original artwork? Or maybe you have a display of antique model cars in a case! Show them off! If your place allows dogs and you have one, take a picture of him laying adorably on the rug. These are the things that make your listing stand out.

- **Photograph of YOU!** While you have the nice lighting, have someone (bring a friend) take a nice photograph of you in portrait mode. You want just your shoulders up, well lit, with a plain background. Make sure you smile, but not too much. You want to come across as friendly and helpful. This will be your profile photo!

It's unlikely that you'll need any **special equipment** for photographing your space. Most newer smartphones take very high resolution photos, so there's not an absolute need for a professional camera. However, **a tripod** can be helpful for getting those nice still shots. And if you don't have good natural lighting inside, you may want to invest in a soft white **photography light**. You can find them online for about $80/100 or even rent them from your local camera shop. If you don't have that option, keep in mind that today's phones' photo applications can really make miracles in post editing.

Complete Outsourcing for Staging, Furnishing, & Photography

A Canada-based company called Fulhaus has taken all of the work out of the furnishing and staging of your short-term rental, and given you a professionally designed and photographed space that's ready for guests in just three weeks with their "Haus-In-A-Box" product.

You pick your style, and they do the rest.

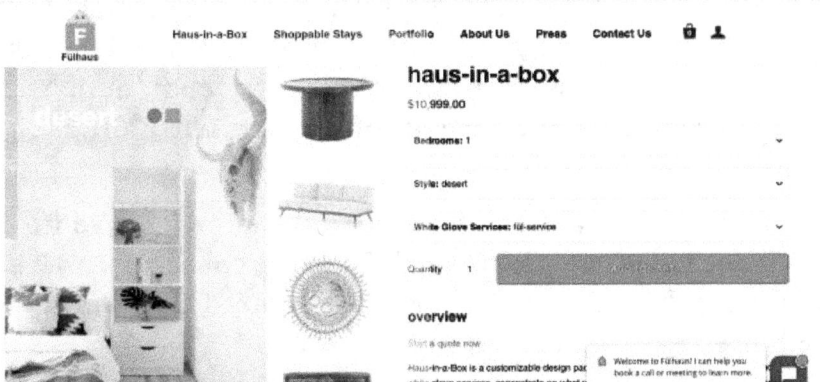

The haus-in-a-box is a one stop design and staging shop that includes almost everything you need to open the door on your property:

Entry (mirror), **living room** (sofa, armchair, side table, rug, floor lamp, 2 cushions, throw blanket, coffee table, console table, 32" tv, **dining room** (dining table, 4 chairs, **bedroom** (queen mattress, queen bed, rug, 2 night stands, 2 table lamps, 2 cushions, throw blanket, standing mirror, dresser, **art + accessories** (2 large framed artworks or similar, 5 accessories, **bathroom** (3 bathroom accessories).

The only things you'll have to purchase are towels for the bath and kitchen, tableware and pots and pans.

Fulhaus offers six different styles as well as a custom option, and their pricing is based on the number of bedrooms. Ranging from $7000 for a studio to $23,000 for a four bedroom house, you really get a lot for your money with this service.

The package includes receiving and delivery with professional photos in less than three weeks.

PLUS they've created another platform for you to make additional passive income with their "shoppable stays" program.

The Shoppable Stays includes a YoureWelcome™ tablet that you leave for your guests and if they love the couch, for example, or the rug, they can click and order one for themselves! You get a commission on that sale. Pretty cool, huh? **You've just created a second stream of income with almost zero effort.**

So, if you don't have the time or the wherewithal to furnish and stage your own property, this service could be worth even financing the extra money that is required up front. It will definitely pay off in bookings!

If you don't want to stage through Fulhaus, or they don't provide services in your area, you can typically hire an interior designer to do this kind of work for you. You can use a resource like HomeAdvisor.com, houzz.com, or freelancer.com to locate the best professional with the best bid.

For **outsourcing the photography**, if you're with Airbnb it is simple. You just go to airbnb.com/professional_photography. Airbnb will connect you with local home listing photographers in your area. These photographers have been vetted by Airbnb and work directly with them on all aspects of the shoot.

Here's the process for an Airbnb photographer:

1. You request a photoshoot on the Airbnb website.
2. Airbnb connects you with the photographers, and you book directly with the photographer of your choice from that selection.
3. The photographer spends about an hour photographing your space, working with you on different aspects of the shoot, framing, etc.
4. The photographer submit the photos to Airbnb.
5. Airbnb chooses the best photos and places them in your listing.
6. HERE'S THE BEST PART: **You pay nothing up front.** Airbnb will deduct the photographer's fee in increments from future listings. It typically only takes a

few bookings before that fee is paid off.

Having said all of this, these photographers tend to be very quick (in that they do not dedicate much time to the shoot), do very little if any post editing, and you only get a limited number of photos. But in most cases it's still better than most amateur photography, especially if you don't feel particularly good at it and do not want to or can't afford to hire a professional photographer independently.

If you're listing with Airbnb, this is a decent way to get a professional look with no money up front. And it takes a lot of work off your hands.

If you're not listing with Airbnb (which, by the way you MUST list on airbnb... especially if you are located in the US), this won't be an option for you. But that doesn't mean you're totally out of luck.

An application called Snappr connects you to a vetted real estate photographer in your area, and the price is right, starting at just $89 for a full location shoot. The page is easy to navigate. Just go to snappr.co and click on "business," and then on the "real estate" tab. Type in your location and get connected!

So, now that you've got your lease signed, your place furnished and staged and photographed, it's time to choose your space-sharing platform (if you haven't already got an idea of what you want to use).

CHAPTER FIVE:
CHOOSING YOUR PLATFORM(S)

Let's focus here on the four major contenders: Airbnb, Vrbo (Expedia), Flipkey (by TripAdvisor), and Booking.com.

Airbnb

Airbnb has over 7 million listings in over 220 countries and regions with 100,000 cities with Airbnb listings worldwide. This platform is probably the most recognized name in niche space-sharing realm leading the pack with a net worth of $30 billion.

Here's how it works:

Airbnb

Guest Fees	Host Fees	Listing Fees
Guests pay a service fee of 5-15% of the booking cost, which covers the costs of running Airbnb.	The host pays 3% of the booking cost. (However, this can vary slightly by country.)	No joining fee, listing fee, or subscription fee.

Airbnb's structure is simple and up-front, and Airbnb leaves you, the host, with the most money in your pocket.

PLUS, Airbnb offers you the security of a **$1,000,000 Host Guarantee** which automatically covers damage to your property above and beyond the security deposit. This is unmatched anywhere else in the travel industry. According to the Airbnb website, this is what's covered and not covered:

What's Covered?
- Damage to a host's property (home, unit, rooms, possessions)
- Every Airbnb listing in every country

What's not protected?
- Personal injury and property damage claims from third parties (those are protected by Airbnb's Host Protection Insurance)
- Damage to shared or common areas of the building that aren't part of the listing itself
- Cash and securities
- Damage caused by a pet
- Damage from ordinary wear and tear

Certain items, including but not limited to: artwork; antiques items, including furniture and jewelry; valuable rugs, collectibles; and other items may have more limited protections under the Host Guarantee.

While the Host Guarantee does not replace standard homeowner's insurance, it gives you a lot of security and goes above and beyond the policy of any other vacation rental site.

Airbnb also provides you with a $1 million liability policy against any personal injury or other claims that could be filed against you as a host of the property. This is at no additional charge and automatically applies at booking.

Vrbo & HomeAway (Expedia)

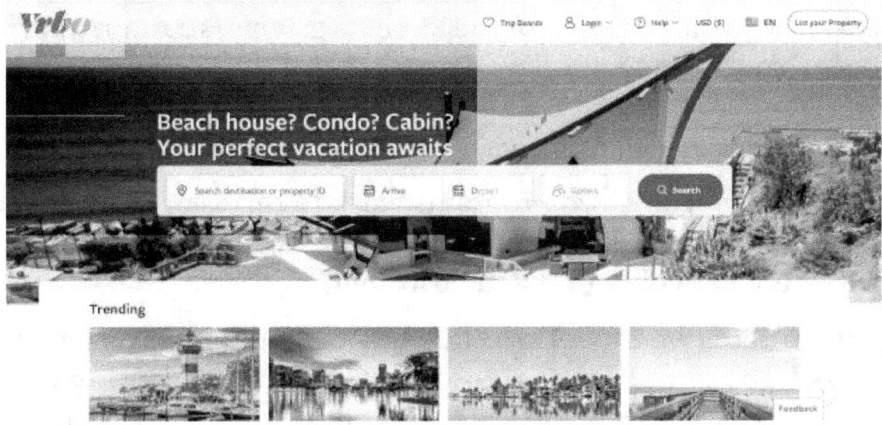

Vrbo is a vacation rental booking platform that falls under the parent umbrella of the company HomeAway, which was recently purchased by the travel booking giant, Expedia.

Expedia, which started as a division of Microsoft, is more like a full-service travel agency covering most facets of travel including research and planning- booking seats on a plane, a rental car, experiences, and more. They have a wide reach in the travel industry, comprising 59% of the global bookings in travel agencies.

Sounds impressive, but what does that mean for your property?

Unfortunately, when Expedia purchased the HomeAway group, they began to experiment with pricing and fees, resulting in a structure that is often confusing for guests and has resulted in some attrition in guests booking on the site.

However, hosts benefit from Expedia's wide-spanning reach. When you list your property with Vrbo, it will automatically be listed on Expedia's Expanded Distribution Network, which includes Travelocity, CheapTickets, Orbitz, Expedia, Trivago,

KAYAK, CanadaStays, and TravelMob.

The benefit of this is that you may reach customers that would not have considered a vacation rental. Having said that, the primary traffic of the Expedia groups is comprised of hotel, travel, and experience bookings... so while you have a wider audience vs. a targeted smaller market, the percentage of that audience booking vacation rentals is lower.

Here's how Vrbo's two programs work in terms of guest fees, host fees, and listing fees, and the overall experience for you as a host and for your guest as a customer.

Vrbo offers two models for hosts. The first is a Subscription model, the second is a Per-Booking model. Which option you use will likely depend on the volume of bookings you expect.

Vrbo Subscription Model

Guest Fees	Host Fees	Listing Fees
6-12% based on booking price	There are no per-booking fees when you pay annually by subscription. BUT, they do charge a **3% credit card fee** on the pre-tax booking charges and you could be charge 5% or more for bookings made through Expedia Expanded Distribution sites.	$499 Annually

This model works well if you have a large number of bookings for which the cost of the per-booking fees would exceed the $499 annual listing fee.

Vrbo Per-Booking Model

Guest Fees	Host Fees	Listing Fees

6-12% based on booking price	5% commission + 3% processing fee + 5% commission (or higher) from bookings made on affiliate sites, + 3% credit card fee	No listing fee

As you can see, the process of calculating the fees on Vrbo is a little trickier and you typically end up with less money in your pocket than an Airbnb booking. However, the high traffic to the Expedia platforms could yield additional bookings.

Like Airbnb, Vrbo provides you with a $1 million liability policy against any personal injury or other claims that could be filed against you as a host of the property. This is at no additional charge and automatically applies at booking. However, unlike Airbnb, Vrbo does not offer a property damage policy.

SNAPSHOT: THE NEW VRBO

VRBO is a vacation rental platform that has been around much longer than Airbnb... so you may say that its two decades in the industry earned them their stripes!

But actually, the striped logo was carefully developed to reflect the platform's new branding-- which is all about the feelings invoked by vacationing with friends and family in unique destinations all over the world.

The history of Vrbo is that it started in 1995 by one Colorado man as a platform to rent out his ski condo. It quickly grew into a space where homeowners could list their homes as vacation rentals. In 2006, HomeAway purchased VRBO, and then in 2015 the company was grabbed up by Expedia for $3.9 Billion.

Now, with over 2 million properties, it is a highly successful company and a good choice for listing your vacation home.

But... with the advent and emergence of Airbnb, the new VRBO needed to refresh their look. So, the first thing they did was listen to their users.

Apparently, a large number of people were pronouncing the name "ver-boh" rather than saying every letter name (which stands for Vacation Rental By Owner). So, they ran with it.

The new striped and swirling logo, with its distinct color pattern, was carefully chosen to invoke all the things the guests love about vacation - excitement, new adventures, and people coming together.

But the new logo isn't the only thing that's changed about Vrbo. They've refreshed their web site interface and developed some new features-- one of which is a custom "trip board!" This is a cool feature that allows you to like and save favorite properties and share them with the group.

This makes it really easy to come up with a favorite rental for the vacation that everyone is in love with!

And that's just one of the new Vrbo features geared toward the customer-- which was exactly the intention! This new site will make it much easier for guests to plan their vacation and book the perfect place to stay.

Booking.Com

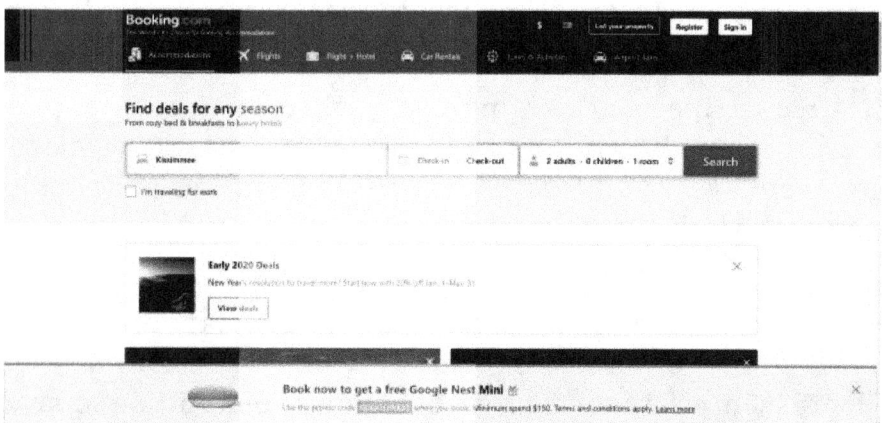

Booking.Com is the most visited travel site in the world. With nearly a million properties, the site books 1.5 million rooms stays each day with NO ADDED FEE for the customer. They also offer a concierge of travel agency services. This can create a lot of exposure for your listing!

However, the drawbacks are higher owner fees, mandatory instant bookings, and the non-exclusivity to vacation rentals.

In fact, their inclusion of hotels in the search process makes looking specifically for a vacation rental home, apartment, or other unique space cumbersome. There is not a search filter to organize into categories, so when you search for accomodations, you get a slew of hotels with a few vacation rentals sprinkled in.

Here is the fee breakdown:

Booking.com

Guest Fees	Host Fees	Listing Fees
None	Average of 15% = 3% credit card fee	**none**

Because the guests pay no additional fees, the hosts foot the bill. Booking.com has the highest host cost of any of the platforms.

As far as property and liability insurance, Booking.Com offers neither. Essentially, the only real benefit to using Booking.com is your listing's exposure to a wider market.

Flipkey (TripAdvisor)

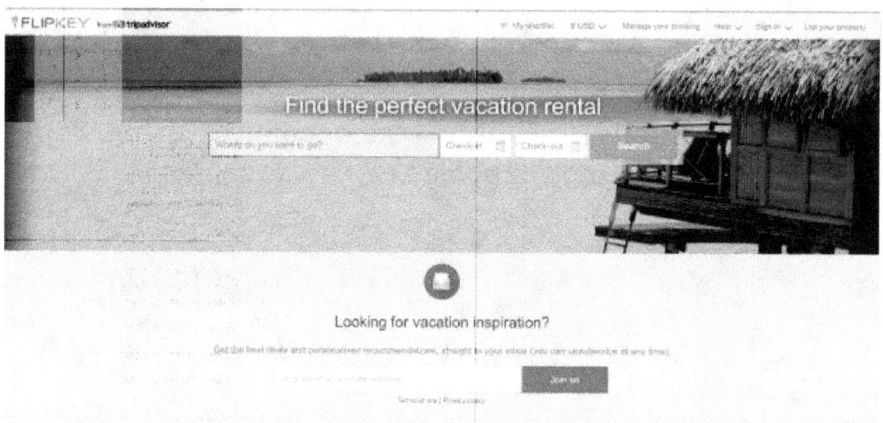

Flipkey is the vacation rental platform under the parent company, TripAdvisor. They have similar features to the other vacation rental companies, only their inventory when it comes to the less popular vacation destinations is only around 300,000 listings, about ¼ of the other popular platforms.

This makes booking trickier for guests, but perhaps could be a benefit to listing your out-of-the-way property... if a guest wants to stay in a small town an hour from a major city and yours is the only listing, you have a good chance of booking that guest!

This is the fee structure for Flipkey:

Flipkey

| Guest Fees | Host Fees | Listing Fees |

| 5-15% of total booking cost | 3% service fee + 3% credit card fee | No listing fee |

While the parent site, TripAdvisor, gets an impressive 145 million visitors per month, it's important to remember that only a small fraction of that is visiting Flipkey.

Another negative is that Flipkey does NOT OFFER any kind of liability or property damage insurance for the host. This information is hard to find, but a quick phone call confirmed. Having said that, you can purchase inexpensive home-sharing insurance through a number of lenders that you can find with a quick Google search.

Now that you have all of the information, you need to decide where you want your property listed… and if you want to list on multiple platforms!

CHAPTER SIX: LISTING ON MULTIPLE PLATFORMS

Listing on multiple platforms is a topic which needs some kind of clear explanation. At a first look, it apparently benefits you more for a short-term burst and then the multiple listing becomes a detriment to your bookings and thus your revenue.

Here's why. The algorithm used in the searches on these platforms is based on the reviews and, for what I am seeing and what has been analyzed recently, on occupancy, or in a few words, on how many days monthly you have booked on that same platform. The more occupancy, reviews and the more bookings on the same platform, the better chance you have of turning up earlier in the search results there.

For example, let's say the first month you book your home on Airbnb, Flipkey, Vrbo, and Booking.Com-- all of the major channels!

You book out your listing for 25 days with this breakdown:

Airbnb (10 days), Vrbo (8 days), Flipkey (5 days), Booking.com (2 days). From that 25 days, you get 3/7 reviews total from guests with their star ranking. The great thing is you've booked out your unit for 25 days! That's a great booking rate for the first month. But now is where the benefit declines.

The #1 factor in search ranking is Guest Satisfaction with the number of guest reviews not far behind. Occupancy on the same platform follows closely. The more reviews your property has, and of course the more stars in each review, the higher your listing will come up in guest searches.

A higher ranking leads to more bookings, to higher prices per night, and then of course higher profits.

If you're splitting your review count between too many platforms, you stay at the bottom of the pile of lesser-reviewed listings and your number of bookings starts to dwindle across all platforms.

So, in the long run your profitability algorithm might decrease from multiple platforms.

Having said that, **if you have a Channels Manager** (SEE NEXT CHAPTER), they can work to maximize the performance of your listings across all channels.

For example, most Airbnb users book over a month in advance. So if your property isn't rented out for an approaching block of time, a listing on another site like Booking.com may fill that blank.

Another advantage of Booking.com is the possibility to get the payment directly from the guests. This means that you can get cash up front for reservations, while all the other platforms require payment the day after check-in. If you have a channels manager, you can set up front payment for VRBO as well.

Your best and my advised option is to utilize max 2+1 platforms to maximize profit, adjusting price to consider the different commissions. You will have to do this manually, unless you have a channel manager...

Which platform to use

1) AIRBNB: with nightly price 100%
2) Vrbo: with nightly price 125%

   +

3) Booking.com: with nightly price 150%

What does 100%, 125% and 150% mean?? It simply means that if, for instance, the price on airbnb is $100 per night, the price on Vrbo will have to be $125 and the price on Booking.com $150. This is to compensate for the commission difference among all platforms and to keep the majority of the bookings (60%+) on platform number one, and justify bookings coming from other platforms only when they give you additional profits or additional occupancy.

The price difference will work to balance the difference in terms of commission of the different platforms and to give the highest number of bookings (maximize occupancy) to platform number one.

The choice between Airbnb and Vrbo as platform number one can be decided by having a look on Airdna, which will tell you exactly which platform gets the highest amount of bookings for each Country, State, City and Neighborhood.

I personally usually use Booking.com to get more profits (with a nightly price 50% higher than airbnb), more occupancy when I have unbooked dates, and to create cash flow, as I am able to charge guests in advance at the time of booking. On Booking.com, this is an option for you even if you do not have a channel manager (which usually allows you to do so with more platforms like with Vrbo for instance.)

Charging guests in advance gives me the opportunity to **create cash flow for months prior to their stay and to have money to invest in other properties. This is a great way to create leverage and add a lot of properties in a short term.**

According to what your goal is for that period, you can choose to maximize profits, or you can choose to increase cash flow getting more long term bookings with short terms advance payments, working on the variable price.

For instance, if you need a certain sum of cash to invest into one property, you can decide to reduce the Booking.com nightly price from 150% to 100% (Airbnb price) or even lower, in order to get cash and make money to leverage on the new properties you are acquiring with that capital.

Furthermore, the AirDNA data shows that listing your properties across multiple channels will ultimately earn them a higher Average Daily Rate (ADR) than those listed on one channel. Why?

One reason that kind of flies under the radar is that most rentals listed on multiple channels are run by property managers and/or are utilizing channels-managing software. This means that they have all the avenues for maximizing bookings in place. Additionally, these properties are often full-house rentals that are available for booking more days out of the year than the single-listing properties with owners that actually live there.

My recommendation is to list your property with at least two channels. And, especially if you have multiple properties, use a channel manager to maximize profits.

So, who... or what... are the channels managers?

CHAPTER SEVEN:
THE CHANNELS MANAGER SOFTWARES

A vacation rental channels manager is an important tool for property managers, especially if you have multiple listings across multiple channels.

The channels manager software takes your property from the photography and description phase into a multi-channel marketing position by listing properties across numerous platforms including vacation rental channels, portals, and online travel agencies.

This may not only include the most popular channels, such as Airbnb, Vrbo, Flipkey and Booking.com, but also the specialty and boutique channels such as 2nd Address, Wimdu, 9Flat, and Homelidays as well as listing sites like Travelocity and Kayak.

With these self-service softwares, you do the work from one jumping point and it distributes across multiple channels.

If you want to remove yourself completely and have someone else do all the work, including fielding calls from guests, that would require a full service channel manager.

A vacation rental channel manager will help to curate your property listings and distribute them across up to fifty partner websites. They will keep the listings in compliance with changing platform regulations and will continually update calendars so there is no overlap.

This means that all information is managed from a single channel management portal, making reservations and any other information quickly and easily updated across all platforms at once.

In addition, a full service channel manager will: create your listing including professional photography, market and distribute your listing across the channels, respond to inquiries and confirm bookings, handle all pre-stay and post-stay communication with guests including requests to review and any issues that may arise, help coordinate local services such as housekeeping, groundskeeping, and maintenance.

The software option makes it easier for you to manage your own multiple listings and their calendars and bookings, to manage pricing and availability from one platform only, in order to simplify multi platform listing, increase occupancy, profits and avoid overbookings. The full-service option employs a team of individuals to fully manage your properties for a more fully automated approach.

These services do come with a cost, and that cost varies based on which service you choose and whether you go with a self-service or full service option.

Top Self-Service Channels Management Software

Kigo

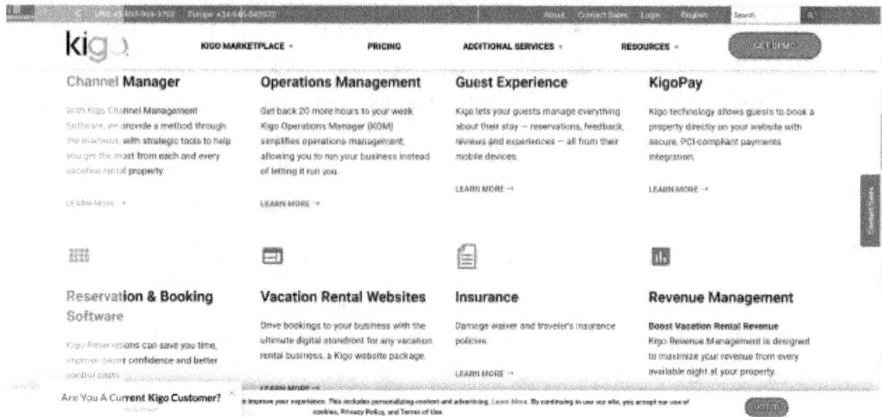

Kigo is a comprehensive property management software that will help you automate your rental properties and save you precious time and energy.

This software will take care of your property information, booking calendars, and guest communications pre-stay and post-stay so you can focus on increasing your bookings and building your business rather than managing the day-to-day operations.

Key features include: websites, operations, owner experience, channel manager, insurance and secure online payment processing.

Included with your Kigo management suite are free trainings and webinars as well as a consultant who will help you implement your program until you are up and running smoothly.

Kigo offers a free 14 day trial (no bookings taken during this time) to familiarize yourself with the software and see if it could be a good fit before purchasing.

COST: $1000 SETUP FEE + 5% online transactions & 3% offline transactions

Guesty

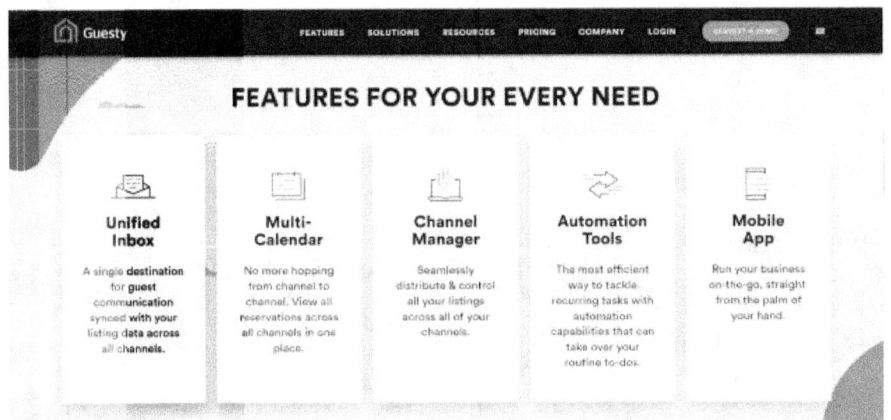

Guesty offers a complete suite of property management tools to help you save time and increase revenue. With the Guesty software, you can manage your listings across all the major channels from one single platform.

With the easy-to-use dashboard you can generate reports, analyze your business performance, process payments, automate operations, and simplify communication across all of your properties and platforms.

Another fantastic feature is Guesty's 24-hour Guest Communication Service, which is one step above simply coordinating channels and organizing data. This service will have a staff member answer all of your guest needs including a personalized sign-off.

Guesty also offers a Mobile App for your convenience on the go, and their software seamlessly integrates a broad range of external management tools to more effectively run your business your way.

Guesty offers a free demo trial of the product before purchasing.

PRICING: Unfortunately, Guesty only offers personalized pricing through an online form with followup communication.

Hostaway

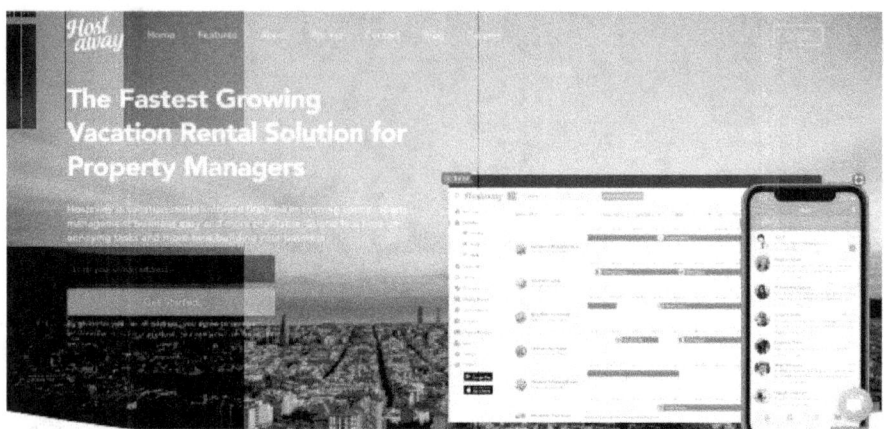

Hostaway is a simple size-adjustable software solution for streamlining your property management. Its suite of applications includes: A unified dashboard allowing you a birds-eye view of your business and revenue streams at any time; a channel manager that integrates your listings across platforms; a beautiful direct-booking website (allowing you to book direct with a credit card); calendar integration; a unified inbox to centralize all of your communication with guests, cleaners, leandlords, etc; an auto-task manager to manage housekeeping tasks; mobile app to manage your business from your smartphone; and a revenue optimization tool to set the most bookable rates.

You can call for a free demo prior to purchasing.

PRICE: While Hostaway only offers custom pricing with inquiry, it is considered one of the better values in the channels manager market.

Lodgify

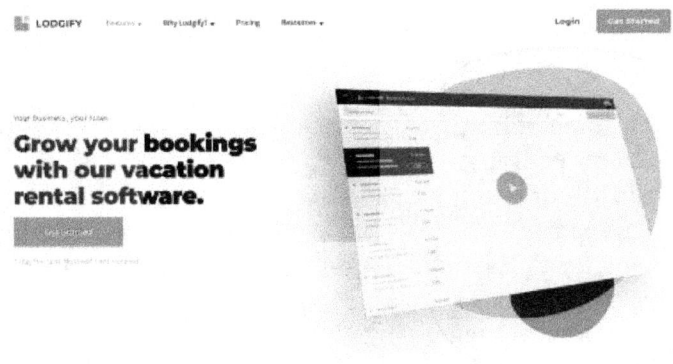

Lodgify is a website-building platform allowing hosts to build customized websites for their vacation rental businesses. It is a complete software package designed to make it easier for hosts, as well as hotel managers and rental lodge owners, to book and manage their properties.

The biggest thing to remember about Lodgify is that it's not just a channel manager. You can actually direct-book from the web site you build with Lodgify, and there's even an option to include your personal contact information to circumnavigate any kind of booking platform.

Lodgify is kind of a one-size-fits-all solution for a lot of different types and aspects of property management. Here are all of the Lodgify features in a nutshell:

- Reservation Management
- Scheduling
- Activity Management
- Customizable Templates
- Design Management
- Credit Card Payments
- Email Marketing
- Electronic Payments
- Email Templates
- Application Integration

- Channel Management
- Multi-Property
- Multi-lingual
- Online Booking
- Room Bookings
- Multi-currency
- Tracking
- Notifications in Real Time
- Web Analytics
- Calendar management

Lodgify is customizable to your business type and size and offers several different pricing options according to scale.

Single Property = $36 per month

2 - 5 Properties = $79 per month

6 - 15 Properties = $124 per month

16 - 30 Properties = $186 per month

31 - 50 Properties = $249 per month

51 - 100 Properties = $336 per month

PRICE: $30 per month with options to customize your plan with additional features. Plus they offer a very basic free version of the software.

As I mentioned in the first part of the chapter, a full service channel manager will essentially take over all of the property management tasks that can be taken on remotely. They will field phone calls, organize cleaning services, deal with guest issues, and more... and that's after fully setting up your listings from photography to listing copy and posting them to the channel profiles.

Here is a solid option for a full service channel manager:

Evolve

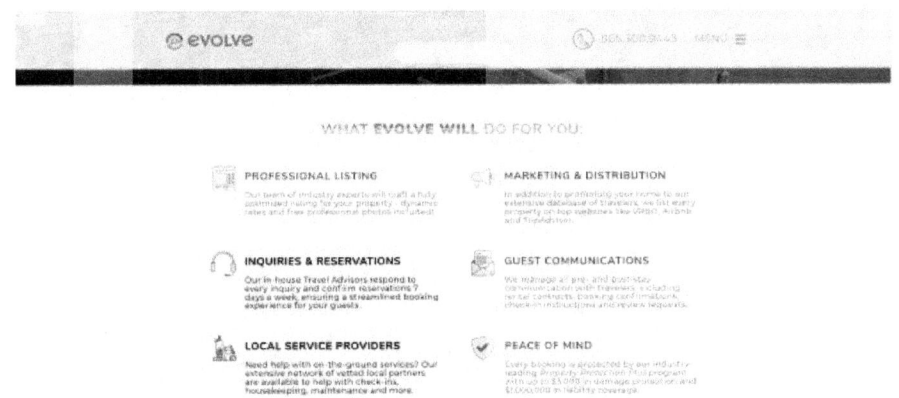

Evolve offers total marketing, booking, and customer support with the flexibility to customize on-site services. The Evolve team promotes and markets your properties, communicates with channels and any booking partners, create nop notch listings including professional photography, respond to inquiries and confirm reservations, coordinate local service providers, and communicate with guests.

This type of full service channels manager allows you to be very hands-off in your property rental business, allowing the manager to handle most of the operations (except filing taxes).

PRICE: 10% of all booking fees.

Before deciding on a channels manager, make sure to ask the sales agent these questions:

1. Do you run the listing on the major channels: Booking.com, Airbnb, Flipkey, Vrbo, HomeAway full network? If not, please list exceptions and any other channels you are linked to.

2. Do you synchronise: Content, images, pricing, availability? How often? And is it a two-way synchronisation for bookings?

3. For instant booking, are you able to synchronise your own payments?

4. How often are prices updated for market adjustments?

5. Do you charge a channel percentage of bookings or a fixed channel fee? What are your inclusive fees and payment terms?

6. Do you connect to any commision-free sites (not Online Travel Agency) where the listing might receive inquiries from advertisements?

Once you get answers to your questions, and you try the demo's of your top choices, you can make a fully informed decision about your channels manager going forward.

Keep in mind, it's smarter to take your time, do your research, and make your best choice from the start because it's difficult to transfer to another channels manager once you've already been using one.

Gateways For Advance Payment & Payment

Processing

Now that you've gotten through the conversation about channels managers, and you're excited to list your properties and start making seven figures of passive income through rent-to-rent, you have to decide on the best way to get paid!

Payment Gateways platforms give you the possibility to receive payments directly from clients, and to receive them even in advance. For instance, at booking time. You can choose your payment policy, which could be 100% payment upfront, or for example 50% upfront at booking date and 50% after check in, or two weeks before arrival etc. etc. You decide yourself the policy you prefer. As mentioned before, this allows you to boost incredibly and quickly your cash flow creation potential, and to have a capital to invest into renting many other additional properties.

In this chapter, we are going to compare features for the four best options for your business-- Stripe, PayPal, Adyen, and MANGOPAY.

In order to do this, let's use Booking.com as our platform, just to make it easier and more streamlined. As I mentioned before, Booking.com is the only platform which allows hosts to collect payments through a third party gateway payment system. Airbnb does not leave hosts this possibility at all, while Vrbo allows that but only through Channel Manager softwares.

With Booking.com, money is sent and received between a huge number of hosts and guests (consumers), with Booking.com itself acting as a middleman, holding the guest's deposit (sometimes the whole amount and sometimes half), and then distributes it to you (the host) has successfully checked into your property (nominally the 15th of the following month counting the guest's check out day). BUT, before Booking.com pays you, they deduct their commission. This is how Booking.com makes their money.

You can easily understand how badly this can influence your cash flow, as you might be paid even 45 days after your guests check out (in case you guests check out the 1st of January you will be paid the 15th of February!) Why not **get paid months in advance for your guest's check-in**? You can see how this would highly benefit your cash flow and possibility to invest into acquiring additional properties.

In order to work for you, the gateway service provider must support the following features: an automated Know Your Customer process (KYC), delayed payout, and split payments. Additionally, your service provider should have tools in place to help handle credit card disputes and tax issues.

Know Your Customer Process

In order to pay money to a person or corporation, there's a process that has to be adhered to that insures the person or corporation is who they say they are-- so the money gets to the right place! Every country has their own laws about the payment of funds, each country regulating this in their own way. But, typically, the information collected includes: Legal name, birth date, mailing address, and ID verification. (More documents could be required in addition to these.)

This can be problematic for companies like Booking.com, Airbnb, Vrbo and other rental platforms because they have a huge number of payment recipients. If the process is too cumbersome or involved for individuals to handle, they may not do it. This is why it's absolutely necessary that your PSP has an option of being fully automated. Easy automation is key!

With some of these PSP, like Stripe, it's so seamlessly automated that you, as a user, may not even be aware that an account has been made for you-- this happens when you provide information like your bank account number and other personal verification information to receive funds into your bank account. The platform moving that money could be a Stripe account.

Other platforms make it blatantly obvious because you have to set up an account before paying or receiving funds through them, such as PayPal. PayPal, for example, tries to help its users by streamlining the process, but you definitely know you're using the platform because you have to physically type everything in.

There are positives and negatives to each type of system.

The first way, such as Stripe, is called a white label experience. This method is quick and simple for the user.

Why? Because if you have to create one more account and memorize one more password, you're going to scream. Am I right?

Having said that, you probably already have a PayPal account... Right, most people do, which means offering this as an option can be a benefit to you.

The other barrier for onboarding providers can be the transmission of sensitive information. Do you get anxious sending your social security number over the internet? Many people do. This is why it's incredibly crucial that whatever platform you're working from (Booking.com for example) makes it absolutely clear that the client information is safe and protected. Who you choose for a provider can have an impact on the client's feeling of security.

That's one downfall of using one of the lesser-known gateways, like Stripe, MANGOPAY, or Adyen. People don't recognize the name, so when the platform lets the customer know that "payments are securely processed with MANGOPAY," it might not do very much to make a customer feel secure about transmitting their information.

While PayPal could create a sense of security with some people because it's been around for a long time, everyone has their own experience with the platform. They could have had a problem with frozen accounts, which would give them a tainted opinion of this option.

Whether it's a lesser-known gateway or a well-known provider like PayPal, customers are often willing to go the extra mile if they see a large potential gain. That's where some of the other provider features become important. Let's take a look at some of those.

Payment Splitting

As an Airbnb host, you do not have to be particularly concerned with splitting payments between parties. Why? Because your platform is going to take their percentage before they ever remit the payment from the guest to you. And the PSP itself will take its cut, too. They all have that feature worked in. Not surprising.

Having said that, all of these top PSP's do have this payment-splitting functionality. Stripe added the option recently where you can split the payment between an unlimited number of parties.

Escrow and Delayed Payout

Most of the vacation rental channels hold the guest's payment until they check in, which means you could be waiting a month or two before you have money-in-hand (like it happens with Booking.com, while Airbnb e the other platforms are definitely much faster). Airbnb holds that money in escrow. This gives both parties security that they will get paid and the service will be provided as advertised. Airbnb holds a license to hold money in escrow.

While, as a host, you should not need to hold your own money in escrow to distribute, if you have multiple businesses with several passive income streams, you may want to look at the escrow functionality of these platforms.

MANGOPAY has an E-Money Issuer (EMI) license, which allows them to offer escrow in all of their countries of operation. With this license, they can hold the money for an unlimited period of time, making them a solid contender in this area.

STRIPE does not have an EMI, but they do offer a limited version of a similar function with their Connect product. While this won't work for you if you need to hold money for longer than three months (in some cases they CAN stretch it to six), if you just need to hold funds for a limited amount of time, it could be a decent solution.

ADYEN does not offer delayed payouts or escrow.

PAYPAL can hold funds for up to thirty days. They compensate for that, at least in a small way, by offering buyer protection. This means that if something goes amiss with a transaction, the buyer might be able to get their money back. But that does not always apply. Because of this, PayPal's security level is not as high as the first two providers.

Taxes

I get it, "taxes" is a four-letter-word-- nobody wants to hear it. But, obviously, we all have to deal with it. And unfortunately, sometimes it can be a complicated process with variations between states.

The bad news is that none of the payment service providers offers its users a complete, comprehensive tool that functions across all countries.

Having said that, if your transaction volume is over $20,000 (and it will be), Stripe has a solid tax reporting tool. It gives you the ability to automatically create 1099-K forms, among other things, which can be a valuable asset when it comes to tax time.

Ultimately, you're going to have to decide which gateway is the best for you and your business. Here's an at-a-glance breakdown of these four:

Stripe (my favorite)

Stripe is a really good option for online-only processing of credit cards and for companies who have the capability (and desire) to leverage the free API for a fully customized e-commerce experience. It is also most likely the easiest to create and set up an account with and the best to use.

Here's a rundown of Stripe's fees:

Credit Card Processing:

 Online Regular: 2.9% + $0.30
 Online Nonprofit: 2.2% + $0.30
 Retail/Swiped: Unavailable
 ACH and Bitcoin: .8% ($5 cap)

Accepted Networks: Visa, Mastercard, Discover, American Express

Fees: NO Monthly Fees and NO Monthly Minimum

Chargeback/Disputes: $15 (refundable if issuing bank rules in your favor)

One of the biggest turn-ons for users of stripe is access to their free API, which allows for full customization of the payment process right within their market website. Stripe works with Airbnb's interface, and it creates a smooth payment interaction.

Having said that, I encourage you to compare all gateway platforms before making your decision. Let's take a look at one of the most known and most popular-- PayPal.

PayPal

As you probably already know, PayPal is one of the most known and trusted online payment platforms in existence. And the most expensive one in terms of commissions costs for you.

Here's how it compares to Stripe.

PayPal is really easy to set up to start taking online payments right away, perhaps easier than Stripe. The downfall is that PayPal sends your customers to another site (PayPal's) for payment, rather than streamlining payment right on your website. However, you can pay for an upgrade ($30 per month) that will allow you to build in payment.

Here's the breakdown.

PayPal Credit Card Processing:

Swiped, dipped, or tapped: 2.7%
Online 2.9% + $0.30
Online (received from outside the U.S.): 4.4% + fee (varies by currency)

Networks Accepted: Visa, Mastercard, American Express, Discover

Fees: NO Monthly Fees or Monthly Minimums / PRO VERSION: $30/mo

Like Stripe, PayPal offers discounts for high volume (over $50,000 per month), or a minimum number of transactions.

The big plus with PayPal is that it already has 179 million

users, making it a common application that people are already familiar with and have immediate access to. The limit with Paypal is that you cannot enter and process manually credit cards number details which are provided by the platforms when the guests book a property.

MANGOPAY

MANGOPAY is a European end-to-end payment technology that provides customers with a fully customizable service that works well with the sharing economy platform.

Here's the pricing breakdown (keeping in mind it is in Euros, not dollars).

Credit Card Processing:

1.8% + .18€ EUR
1.9% + .20£ GBP
2.5% + .25€ OTHER

Networks Accepted: Visa and Mastercard

Clients have 3 months after their production account goes live to exceed 30€/£ in MANGOPAY transaction fees. Otherwise, 30€/£ will be charged monthly until the minimum transaction fees are met.

Adyen

Adyen is a Dutch company that's well-known because it's used by some of the biggest players in the game, including eBay, Uber, Pinterest, Spotify, Microsoft, Groupon, Evernote, and

Etsy. Adyen is huge and international, having reported a processing volume of €159 billion in 2018 (approximately $178 billion USD) in 2018 worldwide.

What makes Adyen a huge standout? It can take payments across all three popular channels-- in person, online, and in-app. This is fantastic for a lot of merchants, but how does it play out for your rental property business?

Here are the stats for comparison:

Adyen Credit Card Processing [from Adyen web site]:

Payment method		Available in	Processing fee	Payment method fee
	ACH Direct Debit	US	$ 0.12	$ 0.25
Direct Debit				(Refunds $ 0.20)
	American Express	Global	$ 0.12	3.95%
Credit Card				
	Apple Pay	Global	$ 0.12	Defined by card used
Mobile				
	Diners Club	Global	$ 0.12	3.95% (in specific situation Interchange++ pricing can be charged)
Credit Card				
	Discover	Global	$ 0.12	3.95% (in specific situation Interchange++ pricing can be charged)
Credit Card				
	Google Pay	Global	$ 0.12	Defined by card used
Wallets				
	Interac Debit (POS)	Canada	$ 0.12	Interchange++
Debit card				(Refunds CAD 0.10)
	Interac Online (eCom)	Canada	$ 0.12	CAD 0.90 with local entity (CAD 0.60 +2.00% for international merchants)
Online Banking				(Refunds 0,30 CAD)
	JCB	Global	$ 0.12	3.75% (in specific situation Interchange++ pricing can be charged)
Credit Card				
	Klarna Pay Later	Nordics, Germany, UK, US	$ 0.12	4.99% + $0.30
Open invoice				For the UK, 2.90% + £0.20

Klarna Slice It Open invoice	US	$ 0.12	4.99% + $0.30 For the UK, 4.99% + £0.20
Maestro Debit card	Global	$ 0.12	Interchange++
Mastercard Credit Card	Global	$ 0.12	Interchange++
Paysafecard Prepaid card	Global	$ 0.12	10-12% depending on industry
Samsung Pay Credit Card	Global	$ 0.12	Defined by card used
UnionPay Credit Card	Global	$ 0.12	3.00%
V-pay Debit card	Global	$ 0.12	Interchange++
Visa Credit Card	Global	$ 0.12	Interchange++

Networks Accepted: Visa, Mastercard, American Express, iDEAL, Alipay, Hipercard, Apple Pay, Google Pay, Elo, Boleto, SEPA Direct Debit and more.

NO setup fees or surprises.

HOWEVER, there is a high monthly minimum transaction requirement of 1,000 transactions. If that requirement is not met, you will be charged $120 USD per month. THIS ALONE can put Adyen out of reach for many rental hosts, unless you have other income streams utilizing the service.

The bottom line here is, do your own research. Check out the web sites, look at the reviews, and in the case of Ayden you can even do a free trial.

One **primary benefit** of using a gateway for payment rather than just using the system in place with Airbnb is that with the gateway, you can get your payment in advance, even when the money is being held in escrow. This option will give you revenue up front to quickly invest right back into your business, allowing you to maximize your passive income streams with a very rapid return on investment.

CHAPTER EIGHT: HOW TO MAXIMIZE OCCUPANCY AND PROFITABILITY

Now you have your property, it's furnished, staged, and photographed. You have your channels manager, and you're ready to start making money! The next step is to maximize occupancy to make the most revenue possible from your listings.

Here are some proven tips to filling up your calendar:

1. Choose A Prime Location!

Hopefully you've followed the steps outlined in Chapter Three and you've already chosen a high-traffic, highly bookable location for your rental property. This is your top tip for high occupancy rates.

2. Get Professional Photos Taken.

Again, you've already followed this advice from Chapter Four and you've posted beautiful professional photos of your property and the surrounding neighborhood. Remember, photos are your primary advertising. Most guests make their first click based on the photo that pops up first with your listing. I can't stress enough-- photos are key!

3. Get The Best Reviews!

Raking in the positive reviews is the number one way to get more bookings on your listing! With Airbnb, the goal is to become a **Superhost**. Once you become an Airbnb Superhost, you'll automatically receive a Superhost badge on your listing, and this gives potential guests the comfort of knowing you are an experienced host with a prime accommodation. To become a superhost, you must: book your property at least ten times annually, have at least 80% five-star reviews, respond quickly to guests (and maintain a 90% response rate or higher), never cancel a reservation. But what helps you get a good review?! Keep reading the tips that follow...

4. Consider The Details.

What could help make your guests' stay more comfortable or enjoyable? Here are the things that guests say are the biggest added value to their stay:

- **Bath products and extras:** Soap, shampoo, lotion and even makeup wipes are things that guests who are flying really appreciate. Plus, a hair dryer and iron come standard in a hotel and guests often expect them from their stay.
- **A welcome basket:** This could be filled with snacks like a bag of microwave popcorn, granola bars, and chips or pre-packaged goodies from a local bakery. It could also be a bottle of inexpensive wine and some gourmet nuts. And here's a tip-- you can add a few dollars this may cost you to your list price, keep them in your cleaning closet and have the cleaning service set them out each cleaning.
- **Bottled water and coffee.** Guests appreciate a few bottles of water, and coffee is one of the most important things that guests miss if you do not provide it. For this, you can have a Keurig or a Nespresso maker (include instructions) with at least two pods per person per day of their stay (or a drawer filled with pods) or a regular coffee pot with a bag of coffee. Also provide sugar and cream (the individual shelf-stable size works best).
- **Breakfast included.** This does not mean that you have to bake three-berry French Toast or whip up omelettes. "Breakfast Included" catches the attention of potential guests, especially busy parents and business travelers, and it can simply mean leaving individual oatmeal packets, a bowl of fruit, and some bottled juices. Prepackaged muffins also work well for a shelf-stable breakfast option. This doesn't have to cut into your profit, either. Just add a few dollars onto the rate. The perceived benefit from the guest will far outweigh the increase in rate.

- **Fully stocked kitchen!** One of the best things about staying at an Airbnb with a full kitchen is that you can save money on food by cooking many of your meals while on vacation or out of town for work. One of the worst things is when you stay at an Airbnb with a full kitchen, but it doesn't have what you need to cook your food! For an excellent rating, make sure you supply your kitchen with enough pots, pans, glasses, mugs, silverware, baking dishes, and small kitchen appliances to prepare all the food your guests will need. To do this, look in your own kitchen (or if you always eat out, look in your mom's kitchen) and see what is there. At the very least you'll need: A sauce pan, a frying pan, a stock pot (for boiling pasta, etc), mixing spoons and spatulas, sharp knives, cutting board, cookie sheets, at least four full place settings and four mugs (depending on the size of the property), wine glasses, corkscrew and bottle opener, kitchen towels and hot pads, can opener, and all of the small appliances (coffee pot, toaster, tea kettle and maybe even a blender).
- **Extra towels, blankets, and pillows.** This will help your guests feel as comfortable as possible, just like they're at home. Having a feel of abundance on the basic amenities really helps you to exceed guests expectations.
- **Indoor entertainment.** Items like board games and playing cards, books, DVD's, ping-pong tables, and premium tv streaming services are a nice touch especially if your rental is geared toward families or larger groups.
- **Outdoor recreational items.** This one seems to be most important if your property is remote and wooded or near an ocean, lake, or river. If it is, guests appreciate the extras like bicycles, kayaks/paddleboards, outdoor games like toss-across and frisbees

as well as badminton/ volleyball nets. While these are not the most important extras to include, they can create a really nice guest experience and that's what you want.
- **Quick replies and follow-ups.** Part of paying attention to details is making sure communication is quick and on point. Make sure you not only reply quickly to guest communication, but that you follow up and do your best to anticipate guest needs. More about this in the "Communication" section and again in the "Automated Emails" section.

So, this basically gets back to the original question: What helps you get a good review? The answer is to exceed guests' expectations and care about every single detail! It's all about hospitality, and the details definitely make the difference.

5. Make It Sparkle!

Cleanliness is absolutely very important to guests… or shall we say, lack of cleanliness will immediately plummet your rating! So, make sure your cleaning service is excellent… and it is by far the most efficient to hire a cleaning service rather than trying to clean units yourself. It is also helpful to have a dishwasher (so guests can load dishes prior to housekeeping coming), dish soap, dishwasher detergent, and a few other household cleaners available to guests so that they can take care of minor spills and cleaning during their stay if they wish.

6. Extraordinary Property Maintenance.

Remember that there's a difference between ordinary maintenance of the property, and extraordinary. When your guests arrive at your property, you don't want them to feel like they're visiting their sister's house that has a couple of kids and a dog. Even if your guest loves kids and dogs, they need to feel like they're walking into a fresh place that's brand new to them.

This means that you're maintaining your property impeccably. Yes, this means having a phenomenal cleaning service that gets every nook and cranny sparkling, but it goes beyond cleaning.

Hire a maintenance person to check on your property every so often to make sure that minor things that would not be reported by guests are in pristine order, such as: Scratches and nicks in paint or floors, broken knobs on appliances, remote controls functioning with charged batteries, door handles and locks are functioning well, air conditioner is charged, sliding doors and windows open smoothly, refrigerator and freezer are running property (including ice maker if applicable).

Create a checklist for your cleaning team and maintenance person with bullet points, and have them send you this checklist signed at every check out. This way you'll make sure they are doing the check-up properly so that they won't forget anything. Ask them to send pictures every time they go to the property, and to do that before and after their intervention.

You can create a Dropbox folder or Google Drive folder in which they can constantly upload these photos, so they won't fill your phone up with sending them by text message or by Whatsapp. This document will make them even more responsible about cleaning and maintenance related issues which may arise as the document will be an official proof of what they checked and fixed and what they didn't.

Also, if within the checklist indicated that something was checked but it then turns out that it wasn't, you will know exactly whether they are doing their job properly or not. They won't be able to say "Oh, I did not notice that."

Always remember that automation and passive income starts from organization and to prevent problems before they appear. This is a clear demonstration on how to automate maintenance and cleaning aspects of the business.

Having all of this running in tip-top shape can make a huge difference in guest experience.

But as we all know, no matter how well everything is checked and working, there will be times when something breaks or goes wrong. This is when it's crucial to have immediate maintenance (within a couple of hours if possible), and definitely the same day. That means you have a handyman on call, or a handyman/maintenance service, that is fully aware that time is incredibly valuable and that they are to respond to these situations immediately.

There is more about emergency situations in the Troubleshooting section, but I can't stress enough the importance of making your guest feel like their needs are being swiftly attended to.

7. Communication.

As in most customer service industries, communication is a major key to a positive guest experience. In order to maintain a top-level of communication with your guests, you want to always reply quickly to questions and needs and follow up to make sure everything was answered and resolved. In addition, you should be sending guests messages to anticipate their needs (remember what we just said previously about organizing the business to anticipate solutions to problems before they arise) - such as messages with wifi codes and lock box instructions, or directions to the beach. This is all covered in greater detail in Chapter Nine: Automated Emails.

8. Adjust Your Rates.

Obviously, you want to keep your highest rates during peak times because you'll be booking out your properties. But in the slow times, you drop your rates to fill the calendar.

There are strategies to setting your calendar rates, and you can also automate this by using a software like

Wheelhouse (for Airbnb), or a similar tool within the Smartbnb channels manager software, which utilizes powerful market data to adjust pricing on your property accordingly.

If you don't want to fully automate (and for the record, I recommend full automation), or if you just want to understand what information they're using to automate price adjustments, here's how (and for what reasons) your rates should be changing:

- **Start low and grow.** In order to get those initial bookings and gain some momentum on your rental platform, you'll want to start your listing a little bit below market value. If you're booking out every day, 100% occupancy, you know you're too low and you want to bring it up a bit. If you're booked out 50% two months out, and 80-90% two weeks out, that's a good place to price your unit.
- **Weekends.** There's a reason that hotels are more expensive on the weekends. If your rates are the same every single day, you're not going to maximize your revenue potential.
- **Seasonality.** Even if you're not a ski town or an oceanside escape, you'll still experience the ebb and flow of the seasons. Figure out what the high and low seasons are for your area and price accordingly.
- **Special Events.** Large events in your area that draw a sizable crowd can book out months in advance and will pay two to five times the regular rate. It's important to keep on top of what's happening in the area and price accordingly.

If, for some reason, you're seeing a particularly open block of dates, offer perks like an extra day when you book four days or a discount for booking a full week. The extended stay is great because your guest perceives an even greater value from the cleaning fee average per day dropping. You can even offer a later checkout (if it doesn't affect your next booking). Guests love all of these types of perks. You get a fantastic rating all around and your property is booked up.

Once you get it figured out, and again - I recommend letting the software do the work for you, you can have your listings booking out 90% or more and maximizing revenue.

9. Consider Seasonal Decorating Or Landscaping.

If someone is looking for a cozy chalet to spend their family Christmas in, photographs of your home decked out with pine garland and twinkly lights with a basket on the counter filled with cocoa and snowman mugs may be just the touch that draws them in. In the summertime, adding some party-style ball lights above the patio and colorful flowers in hanging baskets can make the home feel more festive and like a fun vacation. Just remember to update photos regularly if you can, as you change your property's appearance.

10. Business Amenities.

Fast fiber Wifi internet access is an absolute must, but beyond that, if your property is geared toward the business traveler, you may wish to include:

- a larger desk with a comfortable rolling desk chair
- an Air Printer stocked with paper (and extra ink cartridges)
- charging ports for Android, Google Phones, and iPhones
- an alarm clock

- lint rollers
- paper travel cups with lids for coffee
- pens and paper
- A charging port with chargers for iPhone, Android, and Google Phone

Considering the often-unexpected needs of your business traveler will exceed their expectations and lead to a good review.

11. Think Of The Kids.

If you have a larger house that's geared toward families, consider adding items that will make families with younger children more comfortable, such as:

- A crib or portable crib
- A high chair or booster seat
- Plastic dishes, cups and baby silverware
- Games, balls, and kids' books/DVD's
- A twin air mattress with bedding
- A foot stool in the bathroom (so they can reach the sink)
- Extra towels

Parents will give you an excellent review and return to your property if you anticipate their needs and make their vacations more relaxing and enjoyable.

12. Make It Accessible For Guests With Limited Mobility.

People who need special mobility accommodations look for accessibility as their first criteria on a vacation rental. For your property to be considered disable accessible, it must have the following features:

- Ground floor entrance with no steps, or a wheel-

chair ramp to one of the doors
- Doorways and hallways wide enough to accommodate a wheelchair (at least 32")
- Flat thresholds
- Pedestal or wall sinks in the bathroom that allow a wheelchair to get underneath
- Single-lever faucets instead of dual faucets (they are easier for people in wheelchairs to maneuver)
- Raised toilet and hand rails
- Accessible bathtub/shower or zero entry showe with shower chair and a hand sprayer
- Lower light switches

Making your property disable accessible is one of the more expensive upgrades you can do, but it could pay off in the long run. Most hadicapped travelers will type in "accessible" as their first priority search term, and that will put you in a very small niche market, increasing your bookings.

13. **Create a comfortable outdoor space.**

This is a simple way to make the home feel bigger without much expense. Adding a comfortable seating area outside with patio chairs and a coffee table, a dining-style outdoor table and chairs with an umbrella, adirondack chairs, a hammock, even a fire pit (if you have a yard that allows it), creates the feeling of more space and allows your guests to spread out, enjoy some privacy or gather together, and have a different experience of the property.

14. Offer Local Attractions Or Restaurant Discounts.

This may sound a little cheesy, but people love feeling like they're getting something for free-- a little icing on the cake, so to speak. And local attractions and restaurants often have stacks of coupons and buy-one-get-one offers just waiting for business-owners like you to pass on to their clients. Take advantage of this, and pass the savings onto your guests. Make sure you include the offers in your property description.

15. Install A Carbon Monoxide Detector.

Carbon monoxide poisoning is invisible and odorless, and it can not only make people very sick very quickly, it can be deadly. Many travelers look for the presence of a carbon monoxide detector in the unit. It's inexpensive to install, and not only could it increase your bookings, it could save lives.

16. Accept Pets?

This one is a bit of a toss-up and can go either way as far as bookings. While there are many travelers who are looking for locations that accept their furry family members, you may be eliminating travelers with allergies to pet dander from your guest list. My suggestion is to listen to your guests. If you have a large number of guests who ask about pets, or perhaps if your home is in a wooded area where many people bring their dogs to vacation (hiking, swimming, outdoor recreation), you may want to consider accepting pets. You can always add the pet stay as an additional price. Most pet's owners will be glad to pay a little more for their little friends and you'll have coverage for any possible extra cleaning or maintenance needed. In the meanwhile you would boost your occupancy and profitability rates.

17. Make It Feel Like Home.

Experienced vacation rental hosts, especially on Airbnb, will tell you that often the difference between a four and five star review is the feeling that your space invokes with guests. When people choose space-sharing, they're looking for something special, something much more personal than the generic emptiness of a hotel room. So, how do you accomplish this? Stay in your space! Try it out for a night or two and see how it feels. Do you need some candles, books, art, Kleenex in the bathroom, salt and pepper shakers in the kitchen? What would help you feel like you were being welcomed into an out-of-town friend's home verses unlocking a sterile hotel suite? Add those touches and see how your ratings skyrocket!

18. Hire A Property Management Company!

Your channel management software will cover a lot of management tasks, but hiring a property manager to take care of the hands-on running of the rental unit like screening tenants, taking care of onsite requests and handling emergency situations, checking guests in and out, and even paying and collecting rent. A property management company is comparable to a full service channels manager but they dig into the nitty gritty of the daily functioning of the rental.

Your biggest goal to maximize your profit is to book out your rental properties at the highest rate possible. You do that by being a good host, providing an exceptional stay with incredible amenities, utilizing competitive seasonal pricing and discounts, and maximizing your advertising across the proper channels.

SPOTLIGHT: HOW TO HIRE THE RIGHT CLEANING COMPANY

Hiring the right leaning company can make or break your rating... as if hiring someone to come into your home and get into all the nooks and crannies isn't stressful enough.

But don't worry. Here's how to find the perfect crew for the job.

Go with a Professional Why not just pay your cousin Cheryl's friend Betty to clean the house? She just lives a couple of blocks away and could use the money... Here's why you want to go with a professional cleaning service: Professionals are bonded and insured, they have a consistent and always-available team, they are thorough and efficient.

A professional company can cover multiple properties at once and also provide a fully tailored cleaning plan with a price breakdown. They may even be able to offer discounts for multiple locations.

Ask for Referrals Hiring a cleaning service can be rather easy with a number of personal referrals. So, ask around. Talk to your friends, coworkers, neighbors, family members and compile a short list. Start there. If your property is not where you live, hop onto social media and join the local neighborhood or city page or group. Most people on those types of platforms are more than happy to share a recommendation because they're trying to make business and living in their area better.

Ask Questions Any reputable cleaning service is going to expect you to ask questions, and they will be more than willing to give you answers - because they want and value your business! Some basic questions to ask right on their phone consultation are: How many people are on your cleaning team? What types of cleaners do you use? What is the standard turnaround time on a cleaning? What is your license number and insurance information? What types of services do you provide? Getting answers to these questions will help you feel more comfortable with your service provider.

Get an Estimate Remember, you are charging a cleaning fee to your guests, but that doesn't mean you want to take advantage of them. If I'm planning to stay two nights and have to pay a $100 cleaning fee, that's going to perhaps sway my decision to book with you. You want to charge your guest only what it costs, so get an estimate. That means often having your cleaning crew come do a walkthrough with you, and here it's important to tell them exactly what you want. If you want the beds stripped and all the bedding and towels washed and replaced, tell them. Do you want the dishwasher loaded, run, and unloaded? Yes. Tell them. This way, you're not going to end up overcharging or undercharging your guest.

Trust Yourself After asking all the questions and meeting with your cleaning service representative, you should know if you are comfortable with this team coming into your house and doing a good job. If your gut tells you something is off, listen to it. There are a lot of cleaning services out there, so get the one that best suits your needs.

CHAPTER NINE:
BOOKING LEAD TIME & PRICING METRICS

As I mentioned in the previous section, you will want to adjust your rates for days of the week, seasonality, and special events. Here's a look at three different booking scenarios taken from an AirDNA article, "Vacation Rental Metrics: Booking Lead Time," which highlights the process of adjusting your rates for these metrics.

First of all, what is lead time? Lead time is the amount of time between when your guest books your listing and when they check in. So for example, if your guest books your property on May 1st and checks in on May 14th, the lead time is two weeks.

Why is this important? It's crucial to understand lead time patterns so that you can adjust your rates for the market. Here are some examples:

Seasonality: Antiparos, Greece

Antiparos is a rapidly-growing rental market with a heavily seasonal booking pattern. According to the AirDNA report, "75% of its total annual short-term rental revenue [is] realized during just two months of the year: July and August."

Using the data collected by AirDNA, they see that the lead time and demand has a direct correlation, meaning that the higher the demand, the higher the lead time. They found that the majority of Antiarpo's guests booked their summer rental 17 weeks in advance.

This means that just over four months before peak travel, hosts should be refreshing their listing with details such as proximity to seasonal events and attractions... and getting competitive with their rates. During these peak times, hosts should raise rates to leverage the market and maximize revenue-- and get those new rates on their booking calendar ASAP!

Annual Event: Running of the Bulls

This event takes place annually in Pamplona, Spain between July 6th and 14th. Always. This makes it easy for guests to book far in advance-- and they do!

Again, according to the AirDNA information, for the running of the bulls in 2018, "16% of guests made their event-day bookings nearly a full year in advance." But because most hosts had not yet adjusted their rates, they got their rentals really cheap!

So, the lesson is, when the event is just ending is the time to prepare for the next year!

One Time Event: The Royal Wedding

On November 27, 2017, the Prince of Wales announced Prince Harry's engagement to Meghan Markle-- and the date of their wedding, May 19, 2018 at Windsor Castle. And people started making plans straight away!

AirDNA's data shows that "10% of all bookings for the day of the wedding were made within the first four weeks from announcement."

But then there was another segment of the population that was waiting until the last minute! "34%... booked within the final four weeks leading up to the wedding."

Understanding this kind of statistical information is important to setting your price to maximize revenue. What does this mean? It means that if you had a listing near Windsor Castle and did not adjust your price quickly, you may have had someone book it at 1/10th the market value! The same goes for not adjusting the list price at the final weeks before the wedding.

Because your vacation rental pricing is crucial to its success, it's important that you rely less on instinct and intuition and instead look at the metrics. Fortunately, AirDNA has a new tool that's going to help you determine the prime price to generate the most possible bookings and the highest possible revenue for your property.

AirDNA's Demand Scores

AirDNA's Demand Score is quite possibly the most important piece of data you can have for pricing your rental. Using this tool, you can quickly glance at your calendar and see the lowest demand dates (in darker red) through the highest demand dates (in darkest green), as shown in the example below.

These scores are going to tell you when to price low to drive demand and when to price high when demand is high, thus getting the maximum possible revenue from your rental unit.

This demand score is created from a booking curve based on data about the occupancy rates and the demand booking time over the past twelve months from comparable properties in the area. It also takes into account realtime booking rates on properties available alongside properties already booked. This is going to give you a really accurate snapshot of how to price your unit for market conditions.

This will prevent you from over or under pricing. For example, if you're just hopping onto Airbnb looking up available properties comparable to yours, and you find that they're priced around $1000 per night, you may grossly over price - because the actually-booked-properties average around $260 per night.

The AirDNA Demand Score tool is going to quickly and easily allow you to accurately price your rental, and I highly recommend you take advantage of it.

Another thing you want to keep in mind is a custom minimum night stay for special events - like the Royal Wedding... or the SuperBowl. You're going to maximize profits by renting out your property for $500/ night for three nights, rather than $1000 for one night. It's quick and easy to do a custom minimum night stay, and you'll want to do that for sure.

The bottom line is that it's crucial to keep up with your market and its ebbs and flows so that you can price your listing accordingly. To fully automate this (which I recommend), let a software like AirDNA's Marketminder and the Demand Score metrics, do the work.

SNAPSHOT:
CANCELLATION POLICY

One of the things you'll need to consider when you write your listing is deciding on a cancellation policy. While you may feel most comfortable with a super strict policy, that might not be the best for maximum booking!

So, how should you determine your cancellation policy? The answer is not so short, and depends highly on what type of property you have, the property's occupancy, the booking rate in the area, how new your listing is (yours is brand new), and some other variables.

Based on information from AirDNA, here's how cancellation policy is related booking rate and price:

There are four types of Airbnb cancellation policies.

- Flexible: Full refund within 24 hours (typically) before check-in
- Moderate: Full refund within a longer period before check-in (usually 5 days)
- Strict: Full refund if cancelled within 48 hours of booking
- Super Strict: 50% refund if cancelled a set period of time (usually 30 days or 60 days) prior to check-in. This policy

is atypical and requires invitation.

Vacation Destination

In a highly seasonal vacation destination, like the ski resort city of Breckenridge, Colorado, the cancellation policy on higher occupancy full homes tends to be strict or super strict, while smaller more moderately priced properties lean toward a more flexible policy.

This is likely due to a number of factors. One is that the larger homes (Breckenridge is full of 8 bedroom homes) are typically professionally managed and book year-round for group travel. These groups book out far in advance, so a cancellation would have a serious impact on revenue.

The smaller, less expensive properties tend to use cancellation policy as a competitive tool, setting theirs as moderate or even flexible.

This is illustrated in the graphic from AirDNA's Marketminder (below).

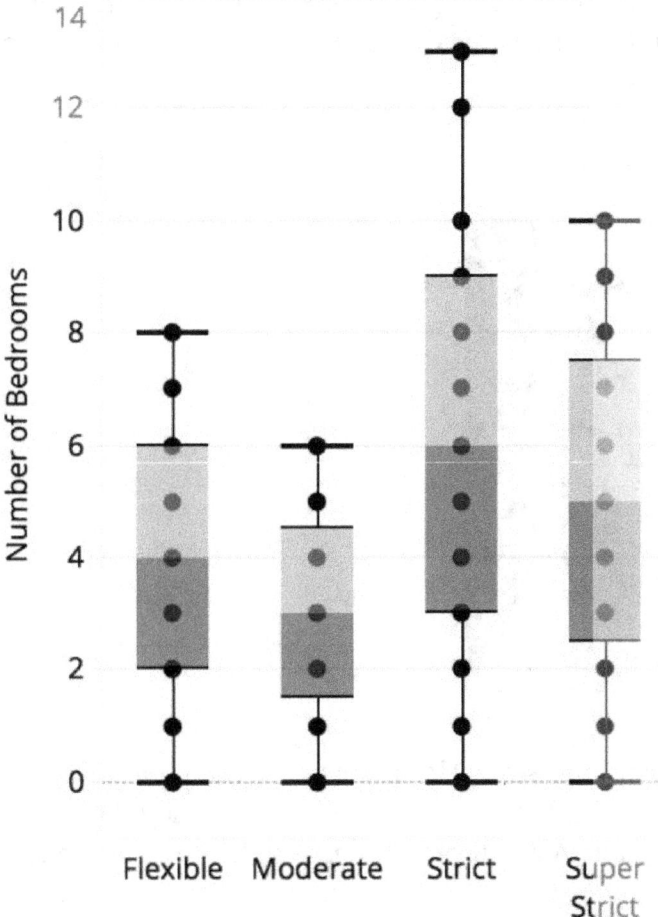

The data also shows that newer listings tend to utilize a flexible or moderate cancellation policy when they first list, and then transition to a stricter policy as their listing gains traction.

Urban Destination

In Berlin, Germany, a city of 3.6 million with a travel industry based on business and tourism, the cancellation policy for

Airbnb rentals leans toward the more flexible side.

According to AirDNA, 57% of Berlin listings have a flexible or moderate cancellation policy. This likely has to do with the nature of the market, which puts them in direct competition with hotels, which have a very flexible cancellation policy.

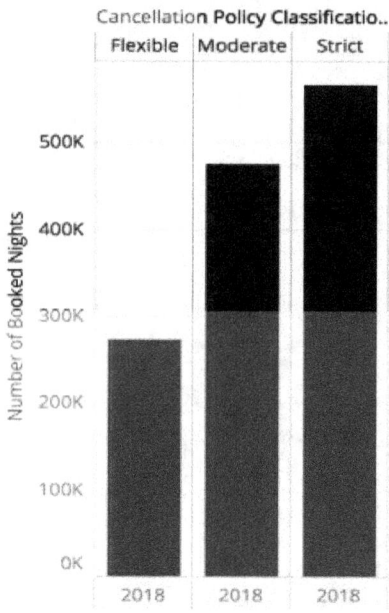

Having said that, the statistics also show that if a host's revenue is negatively affected by cancellations, they don't need to worry too much. A moderate versus a flexible policy has little bearing on revenue.

As you can see in the AirDNA graphic to the left, there are over 500K bookings in 2018 in Berlin with a strict booking policy.

So, with an urban setting, you may want to start out flexible to create a perk for budget travellers who are more likely to look for that option, and then you can always move to a strict policy once you start booking out regularly.

Ultimately, you need to be comfortable with your cancellation policy based on the statistics for similar properties in your area. All of that information can be garnered from Air-DNA's Marketminder.

CHAPTER TEN:
UNIQUE AIRBNB STAYS TO MAXIMIZE REVENUE

One way to attract customers to out-of-the-way destinations, or even just to make your listing stand out amongst the rest, is to go a little bit "crazy" (In a good way, of course) with some unique and in some cases extravagant "houses". These interesting stays will help you increase your revenue possibility and maximize profits with very little overhead or startup expenses.

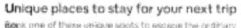

It is absolutely proven that the properties which have the highest rate of occupancy and the highest profits, are the most original and unique ones. In some cases, you would have to apply a Buy-to-Rent scheme rather than a Rent-to-Rent, as it is not easy to find some of these estates for lease. But it would be absolutely worth it as the cost to purchase a yurt, a treehouse or a caravan are far far lower than the cost to purchase an apartment.

From treehouses to houseboats, from tee-pees to castles, you can find a truly unique experience staying at an Airbnb. In fact, the niche is growing to the point where Airbnb has a category just for these interesting stays. So if you're an adventurous traveler, you can click on that tab and open up fascinating places all around the world.

Here are some ideas to get your brainstorming juices going...

Sacred Geome Treehouse, Montezuma

In this sacred geome treehouse in Montezuma, you are literally suspended from the treetops as you walk on bridges between your master bedroom and half bath, living room, and kitchen.

This treehouse is situated on a 40 acre organic farm complete with a farm to table restaurant. It is fully electric with running water and plumbing as well, but you'll feel like you're having a true rustic experience.

This listing books way out in advance, and as I am writing this, appears to have about a 90% booking rate with some months completely booked solid.

This property is completely booked in February and March with just four available days in April. It's already 66% booked in May and the entire month of August is booked. This type of property has a very low overhead for running it, and so it's bringing in a very solid revenue.

"Mermaid" Villa, Bali

In this two bedroom, two bath villa in Bali, your guests are completely surrounded by water in whatever room they might be in, at all times! The relaxing retreat is built on a beautiful pool, and comes complete with giant beanbags to sit on at the pool deck if you want to soak your feet in the sunshine.

The rentals goes for approximately $200 per night and sleeps four, but you have to book out in advance because it has a high occupancy rate and gets filled up quickly in peak season.

La Flocelliere Castle, France

Not exactly something you can rent long term probably (although you never know), or something you can easily buy, but it is definitely worth a mention, for "just" $600 per night, you could stay in the independent pavilion (offering 5 bedrooms and 3 bathrooms) of the medieval tower of this 11th century French castle. The tower sports five comfortable double bedrooms and three full baths and you have access to the beautiful grounds surrounding the castle.

The owners of this property live in the keep, and welcome guests when they arrive. The property is riddled with interesting tales, lore, and tidbits of the region's history.

Because the hosts live on the property, the cost of running their rental unit is not very high above their regular costs of living. And even at an 80% booking rate, with an average nightly rental cost of $600, they are bringing in $14,400 per month in gross revenue ($175,200 per year) - just from renting out the extra space in their own personal castle.

Cob Cottage, British Columbia, Canada

This beautiful earth home is situated on Mayne Island in Canada. Surrounded by woods, it's a cozy cottage for two build with sustainable materials from the surrounding area. It features a nice outdoor area complete with fire pit and adirondack chairs, a cozy study, a full kitchen, an indoor fireplace, and even wifi internet access!

This cottage has five star reviews, it's listed as an Airbnb Plus property, and it's hosted by a superhost. It is the perfect cozy retreat for a writer, a couple, or a small family to get away from the hustle and bustle of their busy life.

This property is completely booked out, every single night, for the next seven months! At an average stay of $120 per night, it's pulling in $3600 per month - which is a good start for a property way out in the middle of nowhere! (In fact, with a rock solid booking calendar, I'm wondering if they couldn't be charging more per night.)

TinyHouse, Seattle, WA

With the introduction of the television show, "Tiny House Nation," people all over the world are wanting to experience tiny house living - maybe just as a vacation or to test it out before they buy or build their own.

And this little tiny house in Seattle, Washington packs more of a punch in its tiny frame than meets the eye. It can sleep four, has a full kitchen and bath and it's own little outdoor seating area complete with picnic table.

The best part of this rental unit is that it is very inexpensive to operate, and since it sits on the owner's property, there is no rental overhead.

Treehouse in Aptos, California

This "luxury treehouse" near San Jose, California has a breathtaking view of the ocean, sleeps six, and is built at the top of a huge tree!

Renting on AirBnb for anywhere from $385 - $700 per night depending on the season, and with a 75% occupancy rate, this unique Airbnb is easily bringing in a revenue of over $160,000 per year.

Glamping, Bradford on Avon

FINANCIAL FREEDOM

Glamping, or "glamour camping" is a new trend among people who want the outdoor life without sacrificing luxury. You can rent these fully equipped tents on an off-grid eco-farm outside of Bath, with no electricity (each tent has a wood burning stove) for $116 per night.

The camp has a main shelter with a communal kitchen and dining hall as well as an indoor heated pool. With ten of these tents on the property, you could be making over $1000 per night. Now, this property is seasonal, but even at an 80% booking rate for five months out of the year, that's a revenue of $120,000 per year (just operating in the warm months)!

Just goes to show, you don't even need a house to start your Airbnb business!

Igloo, Finland

At Lucky Ranch in Finland, you can sleep in an igloo that's almost always negative degrees inside. But, you're provided with a very warm sleeping bag, a real bed, and a warm apartment that's open 24 hours in case you get "cold feet."

This is truly a vacation experience catering to the adventurous traveler!

Houseboat in Bishopthorpe

This beautiful bedroom is not in a house or an apartment or a condo-- it's not even in a building at all! This is a room in The Ark Houseboat Airbnb listing in Bishopthorpe, York.

This beautifully decorated space features three bedrooms and 2.5 baths along with a full kitchen and two lovely decks. It sleeps ten, so you can take the whole family and rest comfortably - for just a couple hundred dollars a night!

The unique Airbnb listings go on from there - including sailboats and renovated Airstream campers. These require very little up front investment and can provide a truly unique experience that many travelers are looking for when they hop on the home-sharing sites to book their vacations.

This profitable trend just goes to show, you don't need a house to have a rental "property!"

CHAPTER ELEVEN:
WRITING THE OPTIMAL LISTING

Your short-term rental description is so much more than a bed count and a rundown of its amenities. Your property description is an invaluable marketing tool and is your first opportunity to connect with your guests.

Make your words count.

You want to write a listing that paints such a clear and wonderful picture of your property in your potential guest's mind that they can't help but want to stay there.

But, you may be saying to yourself as you sit at your laptop, "I'm an entrepreneur, a business person, not a writer. How am I going to write a snazzy eye-catching property listing?"

It's not as hard as you might think.

I mean, you're given a maximum character count and the general topics. It's time to paint by numbers to create a Monet.

Here are the five basic steps to writing a captivating rental booking:

    1. Understand your target market

2. Define your voice
3. Own what makes you special/different/weird
4. Avoid throwaway words
5. Separate your description into property areas

Understand Your Target Market

Understanding who you're selling your product to is one of the most important rules of any business. For your property, the target market is your guest. You're writing this description for them, so it's incredibly important to know who you're talking to.

Go through this list of questions as you imagine you're talking to the guest who embodies the majority of your bookings…

1. Why are you traveling? This is quite possibly the most important question you could ask. If someone is traveling to go to rock concerts at the big stadium venue a mile away, their needs are going to be quite a bit different than the business traveler in for a convention.
2. What do you love about traveling with Airbnb? If the main factor is the homey feel and the connection to a local, that's going to tayler your listing differently than if their main attraction to space-sharing is that they get more space for less money.
3. What's your biggest travel pet peeve? If you can head off things that might normally be aggravating for your guest, you'll be their hero! For example, if it drives them crazy that they can't bring a bottle of shampoo in their carryon and there's not enough room to fit a hair dryer… you know what to provide as amenities!
4. What makes you feel like you've found "your place?" For some people, this might be a beautifully stocked kitchen… for others, it could be that quirky artwork

you hung behind the couch that you found at a flea market… or the pillow with an image of Elvis on

Figure out what drives your primary client toward your property, and utilize those qualities in your listing description.

This may have a lot to do with the location or even the architecture of your property as well. If you're right smack next to a popular business hub, you are likely taylering to business travelers. If you're near a popular art museum, go with the art-lover theme. You're in the middle of Sixth Street in East Austin, Texas? It's a young crowd that loves Tex-Mex and the bar scene, music and nightlife.

Get to know your target market and not only write your text accordingly, but you may want to go back and add some splashes to your decor accordingly.

Define Your Voice

Do you talk to your other the same way you talk to your grandma, the same way you talk to your brother, the same way you talk to your best friend or your coworker?

The answer is "no." You have different voices for different audiences, and writing your rental listing utilizes that same principle.

In the last step, you already took an in-depth look at your target market. So, who are they? How do you talk to them? And finally, how do you write for them?

When people choose a vacation rental, they don't just want to match their number of beds to the number of guests. They want the property to resonate with them. They want it to feel right. They want to find a match to their spirit. (Okay, that might be a bit far, but you get what I mean here.)

The way you resonate with your guest is to connect with them is to write about your property in a way that conveys its essence, or the attitude of your rental.

For example, if you're writing about your beachfront condo with an open floor plan and big sun deck overlooking the ocean, you want to use a breezy, relaxed tone that says, "Come, put up your feet, soak up the sun, put your cares away and enjoy life."

For example: "Kick off your flip-flops and watch the sunset after a day of surf and sand."

If you're writing about a condo geared toward a single business traveler, you'll want to use clear, concise language that says, "We have what you need for a comfortable, efficient stay."

And if you're renting out a mansion in wine country, you want to use sophisticated language that refers generously to "high end," "exclusive," and "luxury."

You want your opening description to tell a story about their future stay that entices them, rather than have it describe the property in detail.

Own What Makes You Unique

When there are tons of options for places to stay, you have to set yours apart to get travelers' attention. You do this by defining your unique selling points early and repeating them often.

Does your property back up to a huge park with running trails and picnic areas, kayaking and fishing? That's what makes you stand out.

Do you have a huge rec room in the basement with a pool table and foosball? That's a big selling point. You definitely want to use it.

Maybe you have a rooftop patio with a view of the city skyline at night, or it looks down over the major league baseball field.

Maybe you have a coy pond, a swimming pool, a covered gazebo?

Or, maybe it's your architecture. Is your property a historic home, a castle, a tiny home, solar powered, Frank Lloyd Wright inspired? Use those characteristics to your benefit.

Here is an example, so I can show you how to highlight your listing's amenities in that opening space. This is a description for a property in Detroit:

Current Detroit Studio Listing

"Fresh Gothic-Victorian nearby the Museum of African American History, Wayne State, Third Man Records, Shinola. Sfumato Fragrances NOW OPEN in the garden level, perfume shop and low-key scented cocktail bar (search for the latest Lonely Planet article). Selden Standard across the street. 9 min walk to QLINE (approx 10 min to Downtown on the streetcar). 10 min walk to U of M Ann Arbor shuttle bus. MoGo bike rental 1 block away. Rocket Fiber gigabit internet speed. Sonos controls in wall speakers."

This studio is in an 1880 historic building. It is a beautiful open space with a huge window offering a stream of natural light. Its full kitchen includes a coffee pot and a nice kitchen area, while the garden level has a cocktail bar. Now, let's refresh this listing…

Refreshed Detroit Studio Listing

"Sip a cup of fresh roasted coffee in the spacious kitchen, or unwind with a drink in the low-key cocktail bar downstairs. This trendy Midtown loft boasts newly-renovated Victorian architecture with a Mid Century Modern flair. Close to restaurants, night life, and the DIA, it's the perfect place to experience the best Detroit has to offer."

Avoid Throwaway Words

The best writing is concise. Get to the point without using trash words that don't really mean anything. Your job is to put a picture of your property into the minds of your guest, to tell a story. Use descriptors that will help you do that.

What are the trash words?

Have you ever asked someone how they are, and they answer, "Good?"

It doesn't tell you anything. So, here are some trash words to avoid: Good, awesome, nice, great, fantastic. Don't use these words. Instead, describe what makes it so good, awesome, nice, great or fantastic.

For example, instead of saying that the property has an awesome view, say this instead:

"The large bay window offers a breathtaking view of the sunrise over Lake Michigan."

Or, *"From the rooftop patio escape, you can experience the twinkling lights of the Detroit cityscape."*

Create a picture in the reader's mind. Boring, throwaway words never grab your audience.

Separate Your Description

The bottom line is that people are lazy. Okay… maybe that's a strong word. But people are definitely busy, and they're not going to pour through your description to find the information they're looking for.

And let's face it, no matter how well you nail your target market, not everyone is looking for the same thing.

A busy family with three kids might be checking the safety information, the bedroom configurations, and whether or not there's a washer and dryer. An art-loving couple with wine and culinary inclinations would be looking for proximity to the restaurants and cultural district.

So, it's your job to make it easy for them to find what they're looking for. You do this by separating your description into sections with bold headings. I suggest the following sections:

- **Introduction.** This is where you curate a solid, clear description of your property that tells a story. You grab your guests with this, so don't make it too long or too detailed.
- **Bedrooms.** Describe each bedroom briefly, but fully.
- **Bathrooms.** Describe bathroom, including hospitality items like soaps and hair dryers.
- **Kitchen/Laundry.** Describe the kitchen, including appliances and extras.
- **Safety and Accessibility features (if applicable).** Describe any special features like carbon monoxide detector, security or alarm system, wheelchair ramp, et cetera.
- **Location.** Describe your proximity to restaurants, attractions, and transportation including walkability.

Here's an example of the best way to set up your sectioned description.

Trendy Midtown Art Loft

Espresso on the rooftop patio, or an omelet barside in the professional-grade kitchen? However you start your day, our bright and airy Boho loft is sure to inspire your Detroit adventure.

Bedroom: The only bedroom is located in the open loft space accessible by staircase from the living room. It has a king sized bed with 1,000 thread-count cotton sheets, a comfortable reading chair with lamp, and large dresser. It has its own smart TV so you can enjoy a movie on Amazon, Netflix, or Hulu while you wind down for the night.

Bed 2: The living room sofa folds out into a comfortable full size bed. Sheets, pillows, and blankets are located in the trunk behind the couch.

Bathroom: On the main floor, this bathroom boasts a deep clawfoot tub, shower, toilet, two sinks, and a huge vanity mirror. Hospitality items include: soap, shampoo, conditioner, lotion, ear swabs, cotton swabs, hair dryer, iron and ironing board.

Kitchen: Fully equipped professional kitchen includes:

- Refrigerator with water and ice maker
- Gas range with six burners
- Oven with convection oven
- Henkel knives
- Calphalon professional grade cookware
- KitchenAid mixer
- Mixing bowls and cutting boards
- Vitamix blender
- Microwave
- Toaster oven
- Coffee pot
- Espresso machine
- Table service for six (including water and wine glasses)

You will have no trouble whipping up a gourmet meal with your Eastern Market produce, or just enjoy a glass of wine and a chartreuserie board, in this fully equipped kitchen.

Safety and Accessibility: The upstairs bedroom is not disable accessible. Safety features include:

- Fire extinguisher in the kitchen
- Carbon monoxide detector
- Building alarm system

Location: This trendy loft is located within walking distance of the DIA, Whole Foods Market, MOCAD, Shinola, and plenty of coffee shops, breweries, and eateries. The Q-line stops just one block away, which will take you down into the cultural district for $3, about a ten minute ride. There, you will find performance venues like The Fox, The Fillmore, and the Detroit Opera House as well as Comerica Park and Greektown.

Now, you get a feeling for this listing and you can quickly find what you're looking for. Obviously, this is not a listing for a family of five with little kids. You can follow these same steps for a bungalow in Washington State or a condo on the beach in Santa Monica.

But now you've got your property well-represented, you're still missing something - YOU! It's vital that you tell the right story about who you are in your channel host profile.

Write The Optimal Host Profile

A lot of people overlook the personal profile aspect of their listing, but it could be one of the most important. Why?

When people stay at a hotel, they're guaranteed that they'll be able to 1, get into the building quickly and easily, 2, someone will be there to help them if needed, and 3, the room will be held to an industry standard level of cleanliness and accessibility.

But with a home-share, they're taking a big chance. They have to trust you, and that can be a big leap for some people. In fact, I'd say for most people.

Your profile description and photo is their first introduction to you. It's your chance to connect with your potential guest, so it's really important that you make it count.

Who are you? You may not like writing about yourself, but for this, you have to. Get into who you are in detail, because the more you write, the more opportunities a potential guest has to find a personal connection. Ask yourself these kinds of questions:

- Where did you grow up?
- Where did you go to school/college?
- What sports did/do you play (if any)?
- What instruments do you play (if any)?
- What do you do for a living/career?
- What are your hobbies or passions?
- What kinds of places do you like traveling to?
- Why do you like being a host?
- What kind of music do you like?

I'm not saying that you have to answer all of these questions in your profile, but this is a good list to get you started thinking about ways to describe yourself.

Use a good quality photo. Very much like your property, your photo is going to give your potential guest a quick first impression of you. How do you want to portray yourself in your business?

- Use a clear photo, professionally taken if possible.
- Shoulders and up
- Minimal or blurred background (portrait mode)
- Smile! You want to look friendly.
- Wear business casual clothing, or at least something clean and tidy that would appeal to all audiences.
- Make sure your hair is combed and tidy.

This may all seem like common sense to you, and that's great. It should. But you will come across some profile photos that make you wonder how they get a single booking (and maybe they don't).

PRO TIP: Ask your professional listing photographer to snap a nice photo of you in your property's living room during your session. Most are happy to oblige.

Verify and Connect By verifying your information, you give

FINANCIAL FREEDOM

your potential guests the security of knowing beyond a doubt that you are who you say you are. There's no reason not to take this step. It's as simple as sharing your government ID, email address, and phone number with the provider (Airbnb, Vrbo, etc.). The information is confidential and will not be shared with the guests, but it will add a verification to your profile.

Now, quickly and easily connect your profile to your Facebook, LinkedIn, Instagram, and Google+ accounts... as long as these accounts are used in a way that will reflect positively on your business.

Here are some examples of really good profiles:

EXAMPLE 1: DAIGO (AIRBNB)

Here's what Daigo did really well:

1. He made it personal from the start by telling us about his wife, his baby, and his cat as well as the small village that he lives in.
2. He talks about his job/lifework/passion - which happens to be building beautiful homes.
3. He posts his information in both Japanese and English (and it's okay that th English isn't perfect, it gives him more personality)
4. He talks about the local food culture.
5. He is verified and connected to his Facebook.
6. He uses a nice professional photo, shown enlarged below.

Excellent Profile Photo

In his profile picture, Daigo is seated in a welcoming position on the porch of one of his three properties, relaxed and smiling. He looks as if he is waiting for you to arrive, and he's ready to help you have a wonderful stay.

Daigo's listing photos and descriptions are just as well done as his profile. I have never met him, but I like him and would feel comfortable staying in one of his beautiful homes. That's the feeling you want to invoke with your profile.

EXAMPLE TWO: MAGGIE (AIRBNB)

FINANCIAL FREEDOM

Meet your host

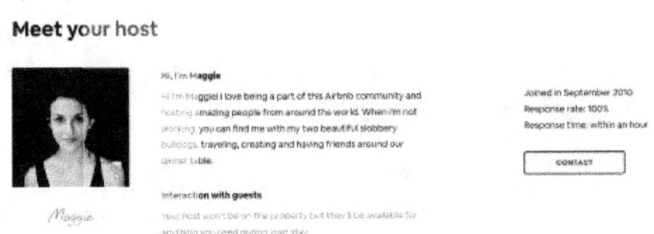

Maggie's profile is a lot simpler than Daigo's, but there are some things I like about it.

1. Her photo is professional and she has a nice, clean look with an open, honest facial expression.
2. She tells us a little bit about herself when she talks about her dogs, traveling, creating, and sharing food with friends.
3. She mentions loving hosting with Airbnb.

If this is all you can muster, it's pretty good. This also shows that Maggie has an awesome response rate and time. It's also not shown in this picture, but she is verified.

EXAMPLE THREE: DANIEL

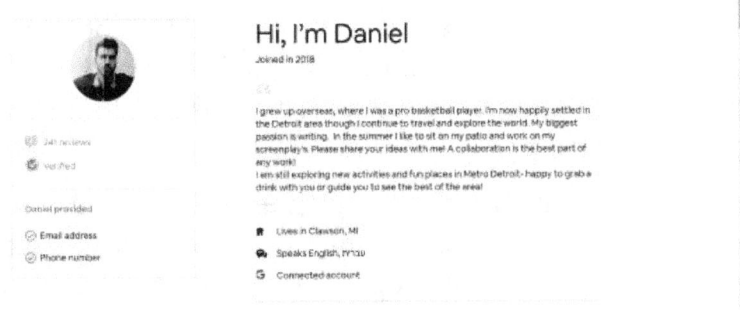

Wow, there is some very cool info about Daniel in the first few words of his profile description. He grew up overseas and played professional basketball - tons to connect with Daniel about here. He also is a writer working on screenplays.

Daniel happens to be a super-friendly host as well, offering to meet up and go for drinks if you want someone to show you the area. You don't have to go that far, but Daniel does a great job making guests feel welcome in his home.

He also has a very professional headshot - although a bit of a smile would perk it up a little. He is also verified and connected on social media.

EXAMPLE FOUR: WHAT NOT TO DO

For this example, I've blocked out the name because I don't want to draw any negative attention to this host. His properties are actually quite beautiful and he is a superhost. But, his profile description has some major flaws - and that's all I'm using it for here.

1. His first major flaw is that he used the profile description to describe the properties more than himself. There are other places focused on the property, and this is not one of them.
2. It's WAY TOO LONG. A potential guest, if they're anything like me, will take one look and skip it entirely. You want to keep your descriptions to 2 - 3 para-

graphs with 3 - 4 sentences each.

3. He doesn't really tell us too much about himself, except he's been in Joshua Tree for six years and done the remodeling work on the properties himself. That could be interesting... but it's buried.

The biggest takeaway on this one is to NOT use your profile space to tell all about your properties. Your property descriptions and photos should do that on their own.

EXAMPLE FIVE: WHAT NOT TO DO, TOO (AIRBNB)

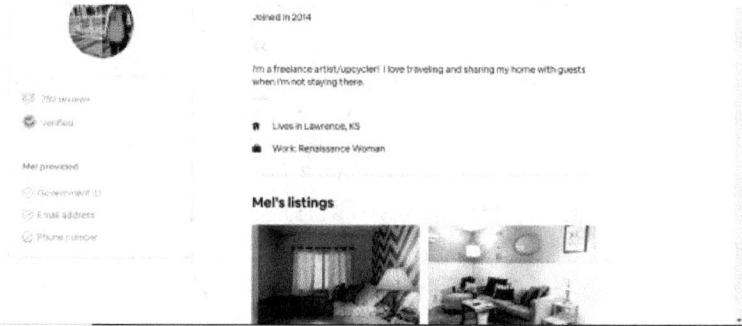

If the last example was too wordy, this one is much too sparse. It leaves us with more questions than answers. Also, her profile photo has her back turned to the camera. Having said that, her tone is light and friendly in the words she did type, which seems to match her listing photos.

I'm not saying that this is horrible, but I do not think it's going to get her optimal bookings on her listing.

Finally, I do want to point out that all of these examples have been for Airbnb. That's because Airbnb has the best and most easily accessible host profiles.

On Flipkey, this is all of the information you get about the host - this is from a listing in Florida:

About the owner: Flipkey

Tim H.
Average reply time: 3 hours 32 minutes
Response rate: 100%
Calendar last updated: 14 Jan 2020
Years listed: 10
Based in: United Kingdom
Overall rating: 5
Languages spoken: English

This is typical of most listings on Flipkey. Flipkey's host description in general is more like host statistics verses an opportunity to get to know your homeowner. The same thing happens on Vrbo, and on Booking.com the hosts are not even listed. Those platforms are all about efficiency, and leave little room for making any kind of human connection.

So, the bottom line in writing the optimal host profile is to tell a little story about yourself and connect with your potential guests on a personal level. Most people utilizing Airbnb are doing so because they don't want a hotel experience - they want to stay in "a friend's house."

To earn that kind of trust and make that connection, you have to allow the potential guest to get to know you a little bit - yes, even if it's not usually you they're going to talk to (in the case that you hired a channels manager and utilize automated messages and a service). It's your job with your profile photo and description to at least create the illusion for your guest that they are stepping into your beloved home.

The often-overlooked bonus of making your guest feel like a "visitor in your home" is that they tend to treat your property and your belongings with greater care than if their perception of your place is more like a "hotel."

A hotel is a big corporation, so who cares if there's soda on the rug, right? But you'd never let soda soak into the rug at your friend's house! Not that it's ever okay to let soda soak into the rug at a hotel, either, but that tends to be the thought process.

Just one more reason to put the personal touches into your profile and spend the time to craft something here that tells the story of who you are.

MY HOST PROFILE WORKSHEET (examples)

Time to write your host profile! Here's a little worksheet to get you brainstorming. The first one (here) will have my example answers, and the next one is blank for you to fill out.

Where were you born and raised?

I was born and raised on a farm in a small town in Idaho.

Born and raised in boston, Mass!

I lived in India until my family moved to California when I was seventeen.

Where did you go to school/ do you work?

I graduated from the University of Michigan with a degree in Urban Planning, and got a job right here in the city that I love.
Got my degree in finance from boston University.

I went to Med School at UCLA, and am now a biomedical research doctor at Sedars-Sinai Medical Center.

What are your hobbies?

I love to hike and kayak, and afterward grab an IPA and a great meal with friends. I'm an avid reader of primarily science fiction (I'm a total nerd), and I volunteer at the animal shelter whenever I get a chance.
I dabble in music production, play piano and saxophone, and still like to listen to music on vinyl - my kids think i'm weird.

When I am not traveling or working, I do yoga and Tai Chi and have occasionally been seen performing in plays with the local community theatre.

MY HOST PROFILE WORKSHEET

Time to write your host profile! Here's a little worksheet to get you brainstorming. Fill out the answers as completely and creatively as possible. This will help you when writing your profile description!

Where were you born and raised?

Where did you go to school/ do you work?

What are your hobbies?

Why do you love hosting with Airbnb?

20 QUICK TIPS TO MAKE YOU A SUPER HOST

As I'm sure you can tell by now, being a highly ranked super fantastic host is up there on your top priority as a new rent-to-rent property manager… and I've given you a ton of information on how to do that already.

But just for posterity, and so you have a quick glance reference, here are twenty top tips to being the best host you can be and making your guests feel welcome and their stay memorable.

1. BE HONEST! Sounds like it should be obvious, but what I mean is make your listing glowing and your pictures great, but don't exaggerate your property. If you have a tiny peak of the lake from between the two houses in front of you, don't advertise as "spectacular view." Or, if your place isn't set up to accommodate children, don't say that it does. Nothing is worse for a guest than to show up and be disappointed. It's a million times better for them to know exactly what they're walking into.

2. BE FLEXIBLE. If you don't have a guest coming straight in the day of check-out, give your guest a little more time. If your guest has one extra adult and it's not going to cause an issue, don't slam them for extra-person fees. If you can, it's always best to show your guests that you want them there and you're willing to bed to meet their needs.

3. PROVIDE SNACKS! Everybody loves snacks, let's be honest. I know we covered this in a previous chapter, but just to reiterate-- little bags of chips, bottles of water, granola bars, dark chocolate squares, small bottles of orange juice... Some hosts even leave a couple of beers or a bottle of wine from a local brewery or winery. All of these touches make your guests shine with delight!

4. ASK FOR FOOD PREFERENCES. I know, again with the food. But people really love it. And if you're someone with food allergies or sensitivities, having a snack you can eat provided by your host really makes you feel like you're getting five star treatment. So, a week or so before the check-in, send an email asking about food preferences or allergies and then leave a little something that meets their needs (which can be stocked in the cleaning closet for the service to leave out).

5. LEAVE NOTES. Small framed notes, or even notes tastefully adhered to the wall explaining how to work remote controls, wifi, tricky lights or fans, and even the shower knobs, can help guests feel comfortable in your home.

6. MAKE IT INTERESTING. Decorate your space with interesting items that show character and give the guest something to look at and admire. If you have travelled or are travelling, pick up small items on

your adventures and use them to decorate your properties... or, decorate with a local flair! Both choices are delightful to guests.

7. KEEP IT CLEAN AND SIMPLE. Now that I said decorate, I am saying simplify. So, the bottom line is to decorate but don't clutter.

8. PROVIDE GAMES AND BOOKS. We have all had one of those vacations where the weather just doesn't cooperate. It's wonderful to have indoor things to occupy yourself when this happens... and as a host, you could provide that for your guests. Fill a bookshelf with all kinds of books, from children's books to young adult fiction to biographies. Then, add a few classic games - checkers and chess are great, a deck of cards, Monopoly, a puzzle or two. I guarantee your guests will love you for this on a rainy day in paradise.

9. GET GOOD LIGHTING! I stayed in a vacation rental once, an apartment in a city. It was really nicely decorated but one whole corner of the living room was really, really dark. A well placed lamp, whether it's in the living room or bedroom, can make a huge difference!

10. MAKE IT COZY. A basket with some throw blankets, an afghan slung over the armchair, a few extra throw pillows on the couch--these touches make your space feel like home, rather than like a hotel room.

11. BE A LOCAL EXPERT! Whether you actually live where your property is located or not, be an expert on local life. The best way to do this is by leaving them a local guide (as discussed in earlier chapters), and sending them automated messages with suggestions for restaurants and attractions.

12. GREET YOUR GUESTS! This does not have to be a physical greeting (although it could be if you live on the property). It can simply be an automated message (with a personal flair) welcoming them to your home just after check-in or just before... or preferably, both!

13. LEAVE FLOWERS. This isn't something that a lot of hosts will do, but if it's convenient (like you have a lovely flower garden or an affiliation with a vendor at the farmer's market), it's lovely to leave a small bouquet of flowers out in the home. It's a nice surprise and makes your guests feel special.

14. EASY IN, EASY OUT. Guests like to check in and out quickly, and this means providing a keypad lock or other self-service key exchange. This is really a must-have!

15. SPECIALIZE IN SOMETHING! Some fantastic vacation rentals have centered around a specialized theme-- for example, a Gamer's Paradise has a full video game console and perhaps some vintage pinball machines, gaming memorabilia, gaming chairs, late night snacks, and more. But if you're going for a theme, go all the way or don't do it at all! You need it to be good enough to attract the market share that would be attracted to your niche.

16. DECORATE FOR THE HOLIDAYS. This doesn't have to be a big elaborate set-up, but small touches to decorate for the holidays make people feel at home when they're away from home - especially for holidays like Christmas and Thanksgiving.

17. PREPARE FOR ANYTHING. Okay, maybe not a zombie apocalypse, but leave your guests

the proper essentials to be prepared for things like power outages and minor injuries... so a first aid kit and bandaids, and some candles, a lighter, and a flashlight are all good things to have on hand.

18.   OVERSTOCK. If your guest capacity is two, leave at least four bath towels (maybe more). Leave extra coffee cups and glasses, extra wash cloths, extra paper towels, extra coffee. Guests will like it if they don't have to wash out a mug every morning or dry off with a damp towel.

19.   MAKE IT SHINE! I know I have said this before, but I can't say it enough-- make sure your cleaning service gets your property to sparkle. Nobody likes to find Cheerios stuck to their silverware or dust on the coffee table. You want it to be cleaner than regular clean, because that's going to make your guests feel really good.

20.   TELL STORIES. This is a wonderful treat for your guests and for you... leave a guest book in an obvious place in the house and encourage your guests to leave notes and stories of their stay. Guests love to go back and look at these stories, and if they come back every year, they love to find their own from visits past.

These twenty tips will make you a super host that goes above and beyond what's required... but what about a "Superhost?

Should You Become an Airbnb Superhost?

Airbnb offers exceptional hosts an opportunity to earn a badge next to their name on their listing, making it easy for potential guests to recognize the best of the best. But is it important to earn that badge?

According to Airbnb, there are quite a few benefits to becoming a Superhost! According to the web site:

Superhost benefits: As a Superhost, you'll have more visibility, earning potential, and exclusive rewards. It's our way of saying thank you for your outstanding hospitality.

Earn extra money: Superhosts often benefit from a significant increase in earnings. More visibility and trust from guests can mean more money for you.

Attract more guests: You'll be featured to guests in search results, emails, and more. There's even a search filter to find Superhost listings. We'll also add a Superhost badge on your profile and listing so you can really stand out.

Access exclusive rewards: You'll get an extra 20% on top of the usual bonus when you refer new hosts. And after each year as a Superhost, you'll get a $100 travel coupon!

Sounds great, right?! But this is coming straight from the channel's web site. What do real hosts say?

Well, the short answer is, yes! Having that badge next to your name gives you more than just bragging rights and some cool bling.

Real Host Benefits of becoming a Superhost

There are some fantastic benefits that come with being a Superhost. One of those is a step up in **customer support.** Whether you're on twitter or on the phone talking to customer support, Superhosts are put to the front of the line and are rarely put on hold. Airbnb is also a customer service organization, and Superhosts are like the elite customers!

Another benefit is a **super filter** that comes with your Superhost status. That means that guests who want to only see the best of the best when searching for a vacation rental can filter by Superhost-- this means they only see listings that sport the Superhost badge!

One of the super cool things about being a Superhost is that if you maintain your status for a year, you get a **$100 travel coupon** to stay at any Airbnb anywhere. That means the host becomes a guest, and that's super fun!

Super Swag is the last benefit I want to mention here, because Superhosts are often invited to exclusive events and given exclusive products - and that's really sweet... Everyone loves swag.

Okay, there's one last last benefit that I need to mention here-- the benefit of booking your property at a higher capacity because people trust a Superhost! When a guest ses that badge, they know their property will be immaculate and everything will run smoothly. The badge is like insurance to your guest (or at least assurance).

So, how do you become a Superhost? Here's the Airbnb guidelines to earn your badge and join the elite society of the Superhost:

How To Become A Superhost

Every 3 months, Airbnb checks if you've met the following criteria for the past year. If you do, you'll earn or keep your Superhost status.

4.8+ Overall Rating: Superhosts have a 4.8 or higher average overall rating based on reviews from their Airbnb guests in the past year. Guests know they can expect outstanding hospitality from these hosts.

10+ Stays: Superhosts have completed at least 10 stays in the past year or 100 nights over at least 3 completed stays. Your guests can feel confident staying with an experienced host.

<1% cancellation rate: Superhosts cancel less than 1% of the time, not including extenuating circumstances. This means 0 cancellations for hosts with fewer than 100 reservations in a year. Rare cancellations mean peace of mind for guests.

90% Response rate: Superhosts respond to 90% of new messages within 24 hours. When guests ask you questions, they know that a quick response is only a message away.

If you are able to meet these markers of customer service excellence, which you absolutely can and should just by following the plan outlined in this book, you can easily become a Superhost in your first month.

CHAPTER TWELVE:
EASY AUTOMATION FOR PASSIVE INCOME

When you atomize your short-stay rental business, it means that you take the tasks you'd normally do yourself to manage your property-- communications with guests, cleaning, opening and closing the property when the guests arrive and leave, calculating fluctuations in list price, and more-- and you make them run almost on auto-pilot. This way, you can focus your attention on other more important things, like travelling or spending more time with your family, working on the great American novel, riding a motorcycle to Alaska... or growing your business, adding more and more streams of passive income as detailed into my first book "Passive Income: From Broke to 7 Fugures in 12 months".

You can even start to funnel some of your capital and energy into additional tributaries to your passive income stream (i.e. fun side businesses), which we will dig deeper into in Chapter Ten!

What does automation mean to the vacation rental business?

Automation is how you take your active income business and turn it into a passive income stream. There are countless professionals out there waiting to do the jobs you don't want to do, and there are highly-rated easy-to-use software systems that are fully capable of doing the rest as well, if not (dare I say better) than you… so why not take advantage of their expertise and these sophisticated tools and services?

Years of training and experience (their expertise) makes these trained professionals good and efficient at what they do, saving you time and money in the long run and making your business run as stress-free as possible. This includes such professionals as freelance writers, web designers and graphic artists, interior designers, cleaning services, maintenance teams, and more.

Here are some tried and true tips to fully automate your business for a passive six to seven figure income while cutting your work week in half, or down to almost nothing.

1. Hire a Freelancer

If you're really not a writer, let's say, you can hire someone for very little money to do things like write your property descriptions for your listing, put together a property guide (complete with graphics), and even write your email and message templates.

Think hiring a writer will cost you a fortune? Think again. You can hire someone to write a full page for less than five bucks. Just make sure to check their ratings and their previous work.

But where do you find a writing professional that's reliable with a proven track record for quality and efficiency?

Fiverr is a platform that lets you connect with thousands of freelancers in minutes. All of the transactions are verified and you can find someone to do just about anything, from graphic and logo design to text and blog posts. It takes just a few seconds to create an account (even sign in with Facebook and there's nothing to fill out), type in your search terms, and get a slew of professionals and their starting fee.

Upwork is another freelance contractor platform that connects freelancers to job listings. However, with Upwork, freelancers bid on the projects and then you select which one to hire for the job. You can interview the prospective freelancer using the platform as well.

If you have a large number of properties, it could be great for brand recognition to design a logo to be used on all of the property communication. Fiverr is a great place to do that.

2. Automating Check-in

It's not often anymore that an Airbnb owner will meet you at the property and unlock everything for you, take you through the building, show you how to use the garage door opener and give you a history of the masonry on the walkway in front of the garden… Most check-ins are automatic and do not even require an exchange of keys.

This kind of check-in is typically more comfortable for the guest with no time commitment from you. In fact, most guests prefer not to see the host at check-in (or really not to see the host at all). There are a number of different ways to accomplish this simple automated check-in:

- Lock Box: This is the simplest way to automate the key-exchange. You simply purchase an inexpensive lock box from the hardware store, install it outside the door and place the keys inside, and give your guest the combination. When they arrive, they unlock the box and use the keys to unlock the door. When they check out, they return the keys to the lock box.

- Electronic Locks (or Keypad Locks): This option eliminates the need for any keys at all. Simply install electronic keypad locks on the door to be used for entry, and set the code. You can also change the codes between guests. Give the guest the code prior to check-in and instructions on how to use it. They will use this code to enter the premises throughout their stay by typing the number sequence into the pad on the door, which will release the door's locking mechanism. This, in my opinion, is the best option for lock automation.

- Smart Lock: This is the most modern and technological approach to keyless entry. A smart lock is a level-up. It will only allow entry to the property when it receives the signal from a smartphone that has been verified. This provides the most secure form of keyless entry. However there are some downfalls to this method. The first is that the guest must have a charged cell phone. This could get mucky if the guest has gone out for the day and their cell dies. The second issue is that they are only for one point of access. Meaning, if you have a gate that needs to be opened before they get to the entry door to the property, you'll need to install two different smart locks.

All of these options allow you to let your guests in any time of the day or night, making it more convenient for your guest and much easier for you!

3. Automated Cooling and Heating

As a host it's important that you are able to maintain a comfortable temperature in your properties for your guests, and also adjust the temperature when the property is not in use. You can accomplish this with very little effort by utilizing a home temperature automation unit. This allows you to control temperature remotely through a computer or smartphone. Here are some popular options:

- Nest by Google: This option ranks the best for energy-saving, making Nest home thermostat is one of the most popular options. This system allows up to six sensors placed throughout your property to comfortably check on and control the temperature of each room remotely from your smartphone. Some of it's stand-out features include:
    - Programmable settings to adjust temperature for lower-energy usage when nobody is home
    - Controls the temperature in each room individually using the Nest room sensors
    - Use the thermostat in each room or the Nest app on your smartphone to adjust temperature
- ecobee4 Smart Thermostat: This is the best choice for individual room temperature control. This system is totally hands-free, as it runs on your voice through Amazon Alexa! Here are some of its best features:
    - Ecobee4 has a HomeIQ which allows you to quickly and easily see how much energy you're using and conserving
    - You're handsfree with Amazon Alexa
    - The system senses hot and cold spots and adjust accordingly
    - Use the smartphone app to adjust the temp on the go
- Emerson Sensi Wifi Thermostat: A cheaper option, this

thermostat is compatible with Amazon Alexa and Google Home at about 2/3 the price. Some of its best features are:

- A traditional thermostat footprint, so there's no repainting when you replace your old thermostats with the Sensi.
- Smartphone app, so you can control the temperature remotely from your cell phone, tablet, or laptop.
- Humidity reading featured on screen for ease of information.

Being able to adjust the temperature of the home before your guests arrive and throughout their stay will make them more comfortable (which leads to a better rating), and will help you conserve energy (which means you save money.) Additionally, you won't have to worry about guests adjusting the thermostat themselves, potentially breaking it or making the house too warm or cold.

4. Automated Emails

This is a fantastic feature you can set up within your email service to provide quick and easy responses to your guest bookings, especially for that initial contact.

Quick and concise communication with your guests is a must for a good customer service rating. Your email auto-responder can include all the crucial information you'd send out to your guests who have booked your property through Airbnb, Vrbo, Flipkey or Booking.com.

The first email should be just to touch base with a friendly "Hello" to your guest. The second message should be a reminder message, the third is a check-in message, the fourth is a checking-up message, and the fits is a checking-out message.

Be sure to personalize this communication so that your guests do not feel like they're talking to an auto-bot. They booked a stay-share because they want a personal touch.

Here's Here are some good examples of automated messages:

Initial Booking Message

Hello Molly,

Thanks for booking your stay with us! We are really looking forward to hosting you in our Ft. Lauderdale beachfront condo. The weather here is gorgeous!

Please look for another email from me the day before your arrival. That will include directions, entry instructions, WiFi password and more.

If you have any questions between now and then, don't hesitate to ask.

Thanks,

Dean

Your Airbnb Host

The next message to automate is a reminder message. This helps ease any guest anxiety about their upcoming trip, knowing that you're there and ready for them:

Reminder Message

Hi Molly,

Just checking in with you about your stay at our Ft. Lauderdale condo coming up in five days!

As a reminder, check-in is any time after 3:00pm. Feel free to contact me if you need special arrangements for early arrival.

I'll be sending you a message with all of your check-in instructions and other important information the day before check-in.

Again, feel free to contact me with any questions.

Safe travels,

Dean

Your Airbnb Host

Your guests like to know that you're thinking about their trip and their comfort when they arrive. These check-in messages go a long way in building a good guest relationship. The check-in message should include the following information:

- Detailed entry instructions
- Directions to the location, including landmark and even alternate routes if it's a high traffic area
- Property policies
- WiFi log-in instructions and passwords
- Any other important information, such as locations of transportation hubs, restaurants, or major travel destinations nearby

Here's is a good template for the check-in message:

Check-In Message

Hi Molly,

Your Ft. Lauderdale trip is getting close!

For check-in tomorrow after 3:00pm, there is a keypad on the red front door.

The keypad code is: 5-7-7-9 #

Type in the code and the door will unlock. Use this code during your entire stay.

The address is [insert address]. The best route from the Ft. Lauderdale airport is [insert route]. You'll see a [landmark] on the south side of the road, and our building is the very next one.

You can park in the covered carport in space number 7.

Free WiFi is available during your stay:

-Username: [username]

-Password: [password]

The Keurig coffee maker is stocked with coffee pods, and cream and sugar is in the cabinet above... in case you need a little pick-me-up after your travel day.

If you have any questions or need recommendations on restaurants or local attractions, please let me know! I'm here to help.

Thanks,

Dean

Your last communication with your guest is typically your checkout message. There are **three goals to accomplish** with this correspondence:

1.   This is an opportunity for you to address and resolve any issues your guest might have had during their stay. Oftentimes a guest won't speak up about something unless prompted, and their silence could end up in a bad review because they haven't given you the opportunity to fix it!

2.   Remind the guest to leave you a review! Let them know that you strive to deliver every guest with a FIVE-STAR experience (make sure you say five-star), and you hoped their stay was a five-star stay (say five-star again). Remember, your business banks on reviews.

3.   Remind them, gently, of checkout time. This is especially important if you have another booking coming in that day. If you do NOT have another booking on that day, and your cleaning service isn't scheduled until the next day, this is a great chance to give them a little gift-- an extended checkout. Let them know they can stay an extra two hours. Your guests will appreciate it, it will give you big star points, and it won't cost you anything.

Check-out Message

Hi Molly,

We hope you had a fantastic stay in our property in Ft. Lauderdale!

If so, we'd love it if you could take two minutes to leave us a 5 star review (it is so important for us, and we would be very thankful for that), and of course we'll leave you the same as well!

If there's anything you need, or any issues that should be addressed, please let us know and give us the opportunity to resolve any loose ends before you leave your review.

We pride ourselves on our hospitality, and our guest reviews are a huge part of keeping our family business a five-star stay.

We value your feedback, and we are continually doing everything we can to make our guests feel welcome, comfortable, and to make every trip a five-star stay.

Thanks again and safe travels,

Dean

There you have it. If you have these templates, your guest communication will run much more efficiently. But, there are a few more templates you may want to keep up your sleeve. These are typical troubleshooting messages, and answers to frequently asked questions. Consider these bonus automated messages:

WiFi Troubleshooting

I'm sorry to hear you're having trouble with the WiFi. It should be in working order, but try these steps to see if you can get connected:

First, try re-entering the password on your device. Remember that passwords are case sensitive. As a reminder the password is: [password]

Next, try resetting the modem, which is located [insert modem location]. Press the reset button and hold down for five seconds. Now, try logging back in on your device.

If you're still having trouble accessing the WiFi,

please let me know.

Thanks,

Dean

Now, rather than typing all of that out, you're simply clicking a button and sending the prewritten message. Most times, this is all a guest needs.

Another question you get a lot as a host is, "Where should we eat?" While it's a good idea to have a manual or list of restaurants at the property, sometimes guests don't want to look at it or just want to ask you personally. Have a response ready for that.

Where to Eat Message

I have a collection of favorite restaurants in the house manual, which you can find on the kitchen counter. But just quickly, here are some you may want to check out:

- [Italian Restaurant name]
- [Mexican Restaurant name]
- [Sports Bar name]
- [Kid Friendly Restaurant name]
- [Breakfast Restaurant name]
- [Vegetarian/Vegan Restaurant name]
- [Walking Distance Restaurant name]
- [American Pub name]
- [Japanese/Sushi Restaurant name]
- [Allergy-Friendly Restaurant name]

If you have any more questions, let me know!

Thanks,

Dean

Another frequently asked question or concern is about your guest's furry friends. If you do accept pets, you'll want a message reiterating your pet policy regarding type and size of pets allowed, where they should take them to walk or use the restroom, and any other pet accommodations that you'd like to mention. Here's an example:

Accept Pets Letter

Hi Molly!

Our condo is dog-friendly and we're happy to make your dog's stay as comfortable and as fun as possible.

Just as a reminder, here are our pet-guest guidelines:

- Dogs under 45 pounds are welcome.
- Dogs must be kept on a leash at all times when walked off property.
- Dogs may run loose in the fenced area behind the house.
- Please clean up dog poop. There are doggie bags located in the bin on the back patio. Used bags go in the outdoor trash receptacle located on the east side of the covered parking.
- Dog bowls for food and water are located in the cleaning closet adjacent to the kitchen.
- Please be respectful of the neighborhood quiet hours from 10pm to 9am daily.
- There is an additional $75 pet deposit that will be returned to you after checkout approval.

Please let me know if you have any more questions! We want to make your stay, and your furry family member's, as enjoyable as possible.

Thanks,

Dean

Now, here's the letter template for when you do not accept pets.

No Pets Message

Hi Molly,

Unfortunately, we do not accept pets on this property.

I'm an animal lover myself, but due to the number of our guests with allergies, the smallest remnants of pet hair or dander could prove disastrous. I hope you understand.

Here is a list of our favorite local doggie camps and pet kennels with beautiful facilities and a staff highly qualified to take care of your furry family members. [List three kennels nearby with phone numbers.]

I hope this helps! Please don't hesitate to reach out if you have any other questions.

Thanks,

Dean

Another template you may want to have on hand is the

followup on review message. Remember, reviews are the key to getting your listing at the top of the search and getting it booked. You want your guest to leave you a positive review. Sometimes, guests get busy and they forget. It's okay to send them a gentle reminder a few days after checkout.

Review Reminder Message

Hi Molly,

I trust you had a wonderful stay at our Ft. Lauderdale condo. If you wouldn't mind taking two minutes to fill out the review, we would appreciate it.

The review lets other guests know what they can expect from their stay with us, and a five star review is the golden standard every host strives for!

Thanks so much, and we hope you stay with us whenever you return to the area again.

-Dean

This should get you started on your automated messages. As I've already stated, prompt and courteous guest communication is key to a five star review. Having these messages ready to go helps your communication go smoother and quicker, especially if you're handling all of your property management yourself.

If you have a channels manager, as I recommend for automating multiple listings across channels, and you've chosen the full services options, you'll set these messages up with them and then they will provide all of the initial contact messages and follow up on guest concerns and questions in a timely manner.

If you are renting with Airbnb, in the messaging section they have an option to use saved messages. This is where your templates will be stored, making it quick and easy to respond to guests via your computer or your smartphone on that platform.

5. Cleaning Supplies/Closet

Keep a locked closet or cupboard in the unit for cleaning supplies and hospitality supplies. This would include any cleaners that you would supply for the guests, including:

- Dishwasher soap
- Laundry soap
- Shampoo, conditioner, lotion
- Window cleaner
- Carpet cleaner
- Kitchen surface cleaner
- Hoover/ Vacuum cleaner (for cleaning service)

This closet should also include non-perishable hospitality items that you provide to each guest, including such items as:

- Coffee, sugar packets, non-perishable creamer cups
- Disposable coffee cups with lids
- Granola bars or other packaged snacks
- Bottles of inexpensive wine
- Salt and pepper (disposable canister or packets)
- Kitchen sponges

Once you figure out how often these items need to be replenished, you can set them up on auto-ship through Amazon. Let the cleaning service know that it's part of their responsibility to receive those packages and restock the closet, and to also keep track of when and how many of the items need to be ordered.

Now, when the cleaners come between guests, they replace the items in the unit as needed and reset the hospitality basket.

6. Concierge Service

Having a concierge service sounds fancy, but it's a really simple way to offer a personal connection for your guests without you actually having contact with them or having to be on site. This works well for apartments or condominiums wherein you can pay another tenant to act as the concierge for a small fee.

For example, one entrepreneur in Austin, Texas runs five listings out of the same building. The units are in a trendy neighborhood full of nightlife and food trucks. It's a huge young-twenties destination. So, he has the tenants of one of the apartments on the first floor act as concierge. You can call them or stop by (during specific hours) and they can answer questions or give you ideas on where to eat or shop or kayak, et cetera. In exchange, he pays them a small fee for making themselves available to do his guests.

I know someone who stayed at one of his properties, and they reported that the concierge representatives were a group of women in their mid-twenties sharing a condo on the first floor of the building, which was marked as "Concierge" tastefully on the outside of their door. Their in-person hours were posted, but their cell phone numbers were made available through the host welcome packet.

These girls gave the guest the best advice about where to eat, where to find cool shops, even which library was the best to go check out on a rainy day. The guest said that every single one of their recommendations was awesome. That interaction alone made the stay a five star experience.

When you are choosing your concierge host, make sure this is someone who knows the area well, is friendly and easy to communicate with, is available most of the time (or can easily set up and list concierge hours), and is responsible. This person (or preferably several people) will act as a representative of your brand, so it's really important to vet them well.

This personal touch gives his listings a more personal feel that some travelers have come to expect with an Airbnb... and ultimately, it boosts his ratings.

7. Full Service Automation Softwares

As stated in the previous chapter, the number one most efficient way to automate your rental properties business is to implement a full service automation software.

The bulk of your management duties fall with guest communication, communication with the cleaning and maintenance services, and updating booking calendars and listings. Plus, to generate the maximum amount of income, you have to also stay on top of the market - which means tracking a lot of property variables including seasonality and special events.

Now, maybe right now you already run one Airbnb... but times that by ten or even twenty. Remember, you're building a business that 's going to bring you a revenue of $1 million a year. Your best option is to implement those automation softwares so that you can run your vacation rental business from anywhere in the world... even the beach in Tahiti, with just a few hours a day.

The automation softwares will significantly reduce the time you spend on repetitive tasks, and allow you to focus on more important aspects of managing your business.

SMARTBNB

Smartbnb.com is an automation software that allows you to craft your own guest experience, fully run your operations on an automated track, connect all of your accounts and streamline communication, consolidate and keep your calendar, and sync and organize your listings across channels.

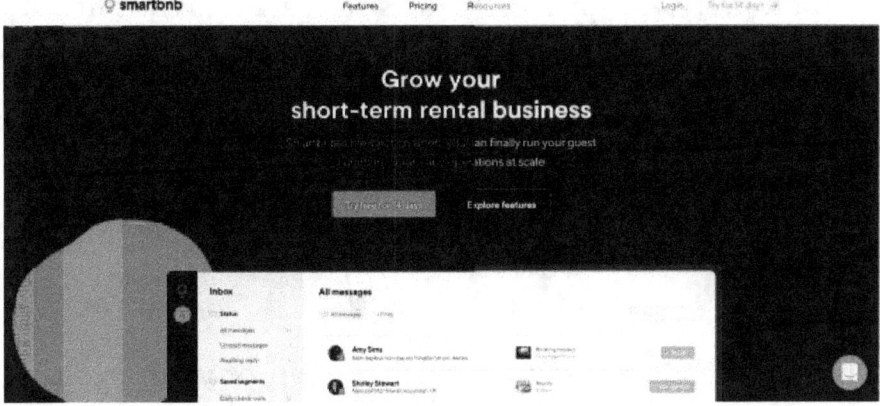

Here's what you get with Smartbnb:

Guest Experience

Smarbnb's easy-to-use interface allows you to completely personalize your automated guest messaging. You start with a simple template for your automated guest messages and you can easily make them your own. With the click of a button, select which message categories you want sent for which properties and when... all the way down to the request for review! You can even have your messages translated into 29 languages!

This is also highly beneficial to your positioning in the platform's search engine. Why? Because you go up higher when you have a faster response rate, and automated is the fastest. Keep in mind that the higher your property comes up in the searches, the greater the booking rate.

Operations

This is one of the most time-saving and incredible things about this software-- it automates the management of the time-consuming task of actually running the physical property. This software connects your property bookings to timed email or text messages to schedule things like your cleaning company, maintenance, check-out visits, or whatever tasks you normally schedule for the on-the-ground operation of your property. All you have to do is delegate, and the software will do the rest.

This feature also keeps your team organized, with shareable work calendars and schedules, group notifications, and more. That means your cleaning crew can pop in anytime and check the property calendar. You can pop on any time and see your handyman's availability, et cetera.

Inbox

This feature allows you to streamline all of your messages into one inbox, and respond from one place with the messages going straight to the proper channel.

PLUS, you can really vet your potential guests and also understand who it is you're talking to with the software's "Conversation Insights" right at the top of the messages. This feature shows the guest's reviews, ratings, distance, and ID verification right at the top of your inbox so you can check it at a glance.

Not only that, but the inbox program keeps everything uber-organized with its own powerful search engine, simple filters, and useful conversation segments and property tags.

Calendar

Smartbnb provides you with a consolidated calendar that you can navigate in real time. This calendar also displays property information, such as pricing, right in the calendar itself. Use a search engine to navigate, and go over reservation details in three different modes-- from full to compact, so you can take a quick glance from your phone or look in detail on your computer.

Properties

This channel utilizes an SEO and listings optimization tool to ensure that your listing gets attention and stays at the top of property searches, which translates into more bookings and more revenue for you!

PRICE: $18 per month for up to two active listings (booked in the last thirty days) with no onboarding or hidden fees. You can even take a 14-day free trial to check it out before you purchase it.

HOST TOOLS

Host Tools is another excellent channel management software that will allow you to be incredibly hands-off with the operations of your business, giving you more time to focus on growth rather than maintenance.

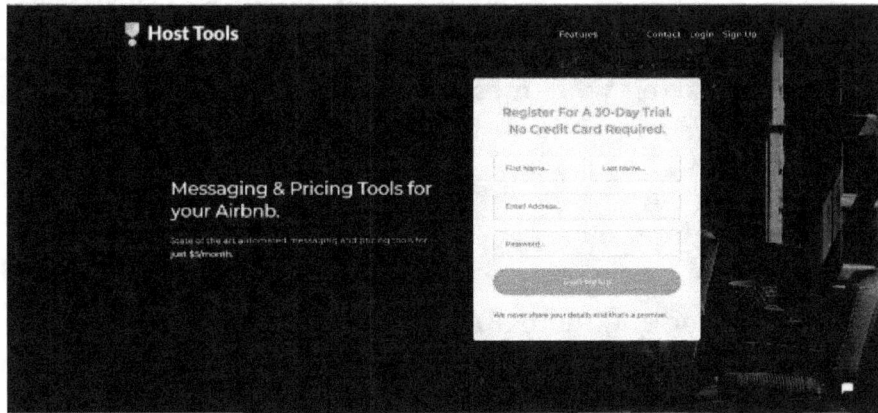

Here is what this software has to offer:

Messaging Tools

Messaging tools are a must for property automation. This software covers all the bases with automization of messages, including the following.

Messaging

Allows you to create fully customized guest messages for everything from initial booking to requests for reviews! You can even personalize messages by inserting guests' names for a more intimate experience.

You can set up guests reviews and instant message them when their review is complete, asking them for a five star review as well. Send last minute messages, booking pre-approval, and follow up on inquiries.

You can even arrange messages to your cleaning service (via SMS or email) reminding them of service schedules. The application also includes a turnover calendar so the cleaning service can quickly access the bookings, check-ins, check-outs and their cleaning obligations.

This product also allows you to group messages by location, which is great if you have multiple properties in one building. It makes management/ cleaning/ maintenance very streamlined.

Fully automating your messaging saves you hours of work every day. It's a must-have for a passive income rental business.

Pricing Engine

In addition to utilizing the AirDNA pricing schematic, you can try the pricing engine included in this software. Their rule-based pricing engine is to be used with Airbnb's Smart Pricing data to give you a list price that's not over or under market value. With this tool, you can also keep your calendar up-to-date and automatically adjust pricing during low and peak times and when your property isn't booking.

Through this platform you can list multiple accounts securely, and streamline your business for automation optimization.

PRICE: $5 per month per listing (includes automated messaging, automated reviews, and intelligent pricing), with an upcharge for additional services. Try it on a free trial basis for 30 days.

TROUBLESHOOTING

So, you've got this smooth-running passive-income-generating business up and off the ground. But as every business owner knows, you will always run into bumps in the road. In this chapter, we're going to discuss some of the problems you might encounter and how to solve them before you get there!

When Something Goes Wrong With A Guest

As a host with multiple properties, you're inevitably going to run into a time or two (or three or four) when something goes wrong and your guest has a problem. Don't stress! You can still get a five star review with a little thought and finesse.

Document All of It

This may sound a little bit uptight and crazy, but photographing (or even better, taking video of) pretty much every square inch of your rental before you ever host a guest is a really good idea (and that will also help you check out the cleaning team standards with the passing of time, therefore you can ask them to do that everytime...) Focus especially on any damage that already exists (please remember that EVERY damage though MUST be fixed as quick as possible, and for sure before any guests check in), like chips in the paint or broken furniture or anything that might pop up later.

Also, it can help to keep a document of where all of your important items were purchased along with receipts and replacement information.

Now, I'm going to broach a topic that can be controversial among hosts-- video surveillance. Some people have really strong opinions about video or not video-- but there are ways to do video that are quite beneficial, tasteful, and can even help your guests feel safer in the home.

There are cameras you can get for around $100 that can be installed outside the front and back door, such as the Blink, which is motion activated and connects to an app that you can view from your smartphone or tablet. This can help you host better, because you know when your guests have arrived... and it will help you monitor how many people are entering and exiting the building, and what they're doing!

This type of camera also helps prevent break-ins, shows you when your cleaning crew shows up, and even when your Amazon boxes arrive!

It will also show if someone is walking out with some of your stuff, if they host a party that's against the rules or gets too large, or if they bring pets that aren't allowed.

The camera outside is not intrusive and, as I said, can even help your guests feel safer in the home. Just make sure you ALWAYS disclose that those entrances are under surveillance.

Another thing to do is to have your cleaning service take an inventory when they come to clean. Count the towels and washcloths, bedding, check for tears and stains or missing wine openers. You can even make a paper checklist for this if you're having a problem.

Automate!

Automation isn't just good for you, MOST guests prefer not to have to touch base with live hosts for things like check-in and out or to adjust the air conditioner. You should remember most of these tips from the last chapter!

Take a Breath

When someone has taken issue with you, they can get rude and they can get ugly and it's so hard to take a step back and be the bigger person. But you have to. You have to be incredibly mature, and sometimes that means taking a deep breath and counting to ten! You just put on your big boy/girl pants and humble yourself.

Remember, this is a customer service industry, and the customer is always right... unless you're prepared with things like camera footage and checklists. If you have those things, your response is simple.

"Dear Jason, I'm sorry you had an issue with not having enough towels. From the front door surveillance footage, it does look like you had twelve extra guests that were not preauthorized..." You see where I'm going with this. Just try not to be rude or snarky. Keep that communication strictly professional.

Be Humble and Compensate!

Sometimes, you'll do something with your booking that is totally your fault. Maybe you didn't get it cleaned in time, or the kayaks you promised access to are locked in a storage unit and the key is missing, or the hot tub was broken by the previous guest. Your guest has a reason to be upset, but if you catch it early and then do something fantastic for them, you can turn it right around. The key word is anticipate and solve issues in advance.

For example, you didn't get the room cleaned in time and it prevented the guest from checking in and relaxing after a long travel day. So, first apologize! Then, to ease their frustration, you have a local restaurant deliver gift certificates (or gift cards) to dine there (make sure it's enough to cover their entire party). Or, you can send a box of muffins and pastries from the local pastry shop. They get a free meal, it makes them feel like you care about them, and you can turn a frustrated customer into a five star review!

Jump the Gun

Rather than being a quick-responder, why not make sure your guests get everything they need before they have to ask? This is much of what we covered in the "Automated Emails" section of the last chapter. Let them know where the best restaurants are with a nicely timed automated message a few hours after check-in. If they already have the wifi instructions, they won't have to ask. Things like that are easy to head off and make your guest's stay that much better.

But when they do have an issue, those premade messages are perfect for a really fast response. Guests appreciate it when you respond right away!

And, if you see that there was an issue, don't wait for them to approach you about it! Some guests won't, and they'll just leave you an undesirable review!

Reach always out to your guests right away during their stay and check in with them to see if there is anything you can do to make their stay even more pleasant.

If any issues have arisen during their trip, even those issues which they do not mention to you but which do not escape your attention, again remember to offer them something complimentary - like if they added an extra person, take that charge off of their bill. You can also offer a complimentary late checkout or you can remove the cleaning fee.

Guests like to get something for their hassle, and you can prevent a bad review and even turn it into five stars!

Use Your Cleaning Team!

I mentioned this before in the book, but making good use of your cleaning team is absolutely crucial to avoiding mishaps with guests. Your cleaning team will come in touch with everything inside the property, so use them to check up on everything!

As I previously briefly indicated, prepare a checklist for your cleaning team including a Wifi Check, Kitchen check (glasses and plates often get broken through normal usage). Have the team make a history of what the average attrition is for dishes and glasses, and make sure you restock these items well in advance, before your guests can complain about a lack of them.

Here is a good example: Your guests check out and your cleaning service sees that the wifi is not working - have them contact your technical service (which is always on standby) to intervene within a couple of hours when needed. Now, the wifi is ready for your next guest.

If you don't have a technical team, make sure your onsite property manager can take care of these issues.

You also need someone to take care of urgent maintenance issues (this could be the same person, or someone else), which are typically plumbing and electric.

With your cleaning team on first watch, and your technical and maintenance teams on standby, you can avoid problems before they have a chance to surface.

Community is Key

Especially if you're an off-site manager, take some time to build a relationship with the community. Let the local bakery, pizzeria, movie theatre and putt-putt golf know what you're doing and make that connection.

You can include them in the directories mentioned in the last chapter, and you can also ask them if they would be willing to deliver to the property for a tip - either food, or gift cards in the case of an apology gift!

When you build your community around you, each helping the other, you can have an incredible benefit and you always know someone's got your back! Plus, it makes your guest feel welcome, like they're also a part of something bigger. That's why many guests choose an Airbnb over a hotel - the personal connection.

When you take some of these measures, rest assured that even when a problem comes up, you'll be prepared to deal with it like a five-star host!

Resolving Guest Issues

The truth of the matter is that you can do everything right, be the best host ever with the best property in the area, and you still get a "bad guest." Perhaps they have broken a piece of furniture, obviously had a half dozen extra guests, or flooded the bathtub and ruined the carpet.

You'll find that most people using the space-sharing platforms are trustworthy, respectful, and just want to have a nice vacation. In fact, some are so grateful and appreciative that they leave gifts and notes for their hosts. However, on the rare occasion that you end up with a "bad guest" experience, there are some simple steps to use to get it resolved.

First things first-- contact Airbnb (or the platform the space was rented under) RIGHT AWAY! You only have 48 hours from check-out (for Airbnb) and that policy is strict. Take photos of any damage, and if the guest refuses to pay the costs above and beyond the security deposit, you need to get Airbnb to intervene on your behalf. And they will.

And remember, your home is also covered by Airbnb's property damage insurance. But that's typically a last resort, as the platform can normally recoup and repayments for damages because they have the guest's credit card on file for such issues.

My second piece of advice on the "bad guest" issue is NEVER to go outside of your listing channels to book straight with the guest. Why? Because you have no recourse against damage caused by the guest and nobody to facilitate a resolution.

Guests may attempt to contact you directly, especially a return guest or a referral from a previous guest, and ask to book directly at a slightly higher price so they can save the platform's fee (like Airbnb's 10% service fee). It's a bad idea. Just don't do it- that's my best advice! Remember that platforms are crucial to this business. It is thanks to them that we can have this amazing way to make money, and they avoid huge costs of advertising which would be needed if we had to run our own channel. Never try to "skip"or cut them out. This is not smart, nor ethical, and furthermore, unfair.

SNAPSHOT: CRAZY GUEST EXPERIENCES!

Becoming a rental host, and being a guest as well, takes a bit of trust on both parts. Usually, it works out just perfectly for everyone involved. But there are those rare times when a guest is just a bit... off.

Here are a few crazy stories of a few crazy Airbnb guests that truly made hosting an experience to remember.

THE VIKING

This one was found on Reddit and it's making the rounds on all of the social media sites. It's the story about one host who got a guest that was maybe a little bit out of context.

"A friend of mine living In Holland had a guest staying from a small mountain town in Germany. Anyway the guy was kind of odd ... with his long brown ponytail and role played viking pretty much the (whole) stay. First odd thing was (my friend) waking up in the morning having his toe tickled at the bottom of the bed by the guest, whilst he stared at him blankly to ask where to find something. Then later on (my friend) went to the bathroom for his usual morning routine only to find the mirror wasn't there. The thing is, this was a mirror that was screwed into the wall ... So he goes to

the spare room and finds the mirror in there. (The guest) wanted to brush and tie his ponytail and decided to unscrew the mirror from the wall with his handy pocket knife and relocate it to the room he was staying in."

Tickled toes? Missing mirrors? A ponytailed Viking guest that wasn't quite aware of proper guest boundaries. The guest obviously wasn't a threat to safety, just a little bit eccentric.

NUDIST SWEDE

The roommate of this young Airbnb host who rented out his room while he was gone, got a lot more than he bargained for when the guest decided that she really didn't want to be dressed. The story was posted on Reddit.

"My roommate and I shared a 2 bedroom apartment had an agreement that it was cool if one of us would be away for the weekend or traveling for work, it was fine to rent out our room while the other person was staying there. We both like meeting people and hosting out-of-towners and are in a great location for young tourists.

Needless to say we've come across some interesting characters.

[One] that stick[s] out:

My roommate was away for the weekend and he had rented his room out to this Swedish chick while my girlfriend was staying over. This girl just absolutely never had clothes on in the apartment. She just walked around in the nude, sat down on the couch and talked to us nude....as if she wasn't nude. When she first walked out of the bedroom naked, my girlfriend and I sort of looked at each other oddly without saying a word. But just let it go as she just carried on normally and chatted with us about our lives, the city, and her plans for the weekend.

I suppose it would have gotten weird if it was an attempt to be sexual....or maybe she was trying something. But it honestly just felt like she was a nudist and didn't think twice about being nude in the apartment the entire time. I had no complaints (she was a looker) and my girlfriend seemed to eventually be comfortable after the initial apprehension (she was sort of an exhibitionist, or at least liked to fuck in discreet public places).

The second night she stayed there, my girlfriend and I stayed out late, so the Swedish girl beat us home and returned to her just sitting on the couch naked, watching TV."

A nudist guest maybe should have asked, or shared that information, before they stripped down to watch TV. But in the end, it was harmless and it made for a really good story.

While most of the bizarre guest stories are just bizarre, a few get out of hand and the host has to get the Airbnb staff involved to help handle it (which they do).

There's one story where a woman rented out her vacation home on Airbnb for $1450 per month to a young male guest. It turns out, she came across her own home as a listing and discovered that the guest had been listing it himself on Airbnb for hundreds of dollars a night! And when she tried to address it, he refused to leave.

So, the frustrated host booked the listing herself and when she got in, she changed the locks!

Of course, this is a strange guest experience and one that's very rare in the host world. But trust me, there are also strange hosts out there too (just make sure you're not one of them).

ALIEN ABDUCTION

A guest rented a room in a house in Colorado when she got the job of her dreams. She thought she'd Airbnb for a month to save some money and look for a place. But when she arrived, she realized her host was a little wacky-- she was absolutely sure she'd been abducted by aliens. The behavior grew increasingly worse, sometimes going up on the roof to look for signs.

I wonder if her booking came with a free tin foil hat? Needless to say, there were no encounters with UFO's... just a strange encounter with a crazy host.

URBAN IGLOO

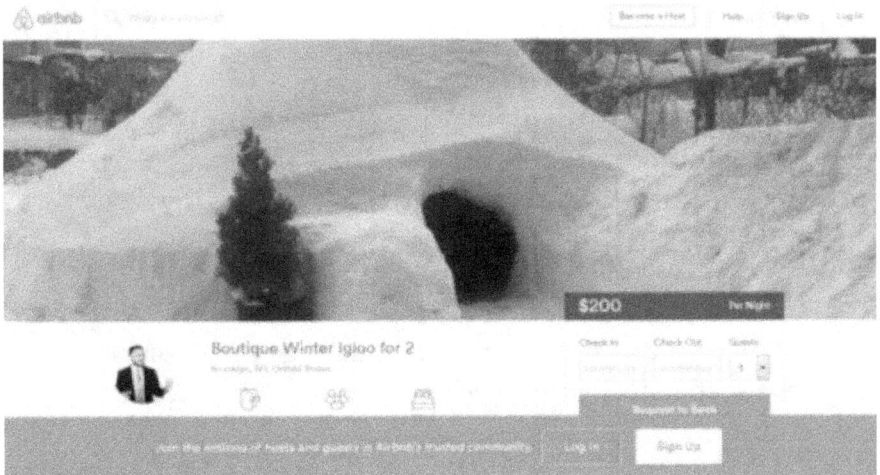

Another crazy host decided to build an igloo in his backyard in Brooklyn, New YOrk and list it on Airbnb for $200 a night! No beds or pillows, no bathroom... just snow. An urban adventure? Or a frigid nightmare? No worries, Airbnb took down the listing before he could book a guest. It didn't quite meet the hospitality standards for an Airbnb property.

HOW TO STAY BED BUG FREE

Bed bugs are microscopic bugs that latch onto people and bedding and infiltrate mattresses. They are attracted to your body heat and bite when you're asleep, leaving tiny itchy bites on your skin.

And once they're in, they're really hard to get rid of!

Unfortunately, as a rental property manager these pesky little bugs are something you're going to need to be aware of-- and make sure they're not infesting your home!

Nothing says a zero-star rating like a bed bug infestation! Not only that, but a bed bug infestation will shut down your rental property until it's been thoroughly fumigated.

Here's how to prevent that from happening from the start, because as you know, an ounce of prevention is worth a pound of cure.

1. **Provide Dirty Laundry Hampers:** Something a lot of people don't realize is that bed bugs are really attracted to dirty laundry - maybe even more so to the mattresses. They also come in on people's clothing and bodies and that's how they spread. So, if you

provide a lidded laundry hamper in the bathroom or hallway, or even in the bedroom as far away from the bed as possible, guests are more likely to drop their soiled clothes or towels in there rather than tossing them on the bed or floor near the bed.

2. **Zip Up Your Mattresses:** The best way to protect your mattresses (and ultimately, your guests) from bedbugs is to zip your mattress into a bed-bug barrier mattress case. This is less permeable than a traditional mattress topper, which is typically made out of cloth. But remember, you still want your guest to get an incredible sleep experience, so do NOT choose a plastic mattress cover. While plastic will, indeed, keep the pests out of your bed, it will also crinkle and slide beneath the sheets-- this makes for a horrible sleep experience. Instead, choose a good thick-knitted polyester fabric cover that zips tight to your mattress without much slack. This way, your sheets won't slide around when your guest tosses and turns. Adding a mattress protector will not only save you from a bed bug infestation, it can protect from spills and bed wetting as well.

3. **Clean, Clean and More Clean!** Make sure your cleaning service is vacuuming all carpets and cleaning all rugs well in the bedroom areas (as well as the rest of the house). This will prevent the bed bugs from traveling in, or traveling from one area of the house to another.

While bed bugs can be an enormous headache, they can also easily be avoided with a few simple precautions.

DO NOT LET THIS HAPPEN (EVER)

While I completely understand that as you get started on this journey, you are learning, and you are bound to make a few mistakes. And that's forgivable. BUT, there are a few mistakes that are easily avoidable, and that you should NEVER allow to happen with your properties.

Do you understand, I mean NEVER.

There are no excuses for these next five huge host blunders (that will leave your guests fuming, and giving you two stars).

NEVER Mistake Number One: Not enough towels. Most people do not typically travel with their own towels. In fact, I'd dare say that nobody does. You need to stock PLENTY of bath towels, at least two (but I would warm recommend at least three or even four...) per occupancy capacity. If there's not a lot of room in the bathroom, you can leave a stack in the linen closet, on a dresser, or on the washer or dryer. Just make sure there are enough so that your guests do not run out or have to use a wet towel. This also goes for washcloths and kitchen towels. Also, if your property has a pool or spa, or is near the beach, you should consider also stocking a number of beach towels so that your bath towels do not get ruined from going in and out of the house and used with chlorinated or salt water.

NEVER Mistake Number Two: Locked out! In this age of technology (and even simple gadgets) there is never any reason at all for your guest to get locked out of the property (or not to be able to get in to begin with). First, you can use a keypad lock with a code. This is the easiest solution (prevention), and make sure you send the code multiple times to your guest prior to arrival. If you do not use a keypad lock, and you prefer a traditional key, make sure your lock box is easy to open... and leave an extra key in another lock box on the property in case of emergencies! Let your guest know where that emergency key is in their check-in instructions. You can also avoid lock-outs by giving your guests more than one key to begin with - especially if there will be more than one guest staying.

NEVER Mistake Number Three: Invasion of privacy. Unless you're renting out a room in your house that you're living in, most guests do not expect to see you during their stay. At all. They want this time to be private, like a traditional vacation rental property or hospitality suite... unless they book a room in your home, which is another story entirely.

But with a full unit booking, barring some kind of emergency (including fire, flood, or other major catastrophe), stay away from the property while your guests are there. This also includes the cleaning service, maintenance, and tech crew. Of course, that is, unless the toilet overflows or the wifi really and truly won't connect-- then by all means, ask your guest if they mind the team coming straight away to fix it.

NEVER Mistake Number Four: Missing Amenities. Everything you advertise in your listing should be there for your guest, with no exceptions. If you say you have a coffee pot, and your guests show up and they realize there's no way to make a cup of coffee, you're going to end up with one star for sure! (Guests are very serious about their coffee.)

I know it sounds crazy, but guests pour through the listings across several platforms, sometimes taking days or weeks to choose their perfect vacation rental. How do they determine where they want to stay? Guests largely base their choices on the amenities that best meet their needs, after they get the proper number of beds and the right location. So, amenities listed are very important. I mean, if your guest expects a hair dryer, so they don't pack one… bad hair for the whole vacation will make your guest rather cranky. All this requires is for you to keep to your word, and have that cleaning service go through the checklist every time, as I said in the previous section.

As you probably understand, this is not a conclusive list-- but these right here are five big no-no's that you can easily avoid to ensure a happy, five star experience for every guest at your properties.

NEVER Mistake Number Five: No toilet paper! There is rarely a more vulnerable feeling than being in the bathroom (or just having to go) and realizing there is no more toilet paper left. This doesn't just mean that you need to make sure there's paper on the roll. You need to make sure there is plenty of toilet paper in the house to last your guests their entire stay, plus another lifetime. This is one of those items that you should have on Amazon auto-order. Keep it stocked in your linen closet and your cleaning closet, and instruct your cleaning crew to place plenty of rolls within reach of every toilet. As an addendum… this also includes napkins and paper towels (only, keep those in the kitchen).

CHAPTER THIRTEEN:
ADDITIONAL AIRBNB-RELATED INCOME STREAMS

Now that you have your primary passive income stream up and running as smoothly as possible, and its generating a sizable passive income, there's no reason not to additional income to the mix.

This would be a good time to revisit the goals you set for yourself when you started your rental income business. Are you hitting those goals? Did you surpass them?

Maybe you're hitting your original fiscal goals, but you haven't taken that trip to Bali that was a part of your lifestyle goals timeline because you quit your full time job by replacing all of your income with rent-to-rent revenue, but you don't quite have enough extra for the kind of trip you've been dreaming of!

Well, now's your time. You can make that goal a reality!

You can make as much money as you want to make using this model of passive income! Your earning potential is only limited by your imagination and willingness to try.

Here are some tried-and-true smaller tributaries to your income stream that pair seamlessly with your rent-to-rent business.

- Amazon Affiliate
- Travel Guides
- Kayak/jet ski/canoe and bicycle
- Local Guide Ad Sales
- Car Share
- Small Business Partnerships (MLM and local)
- Open Laundry/Laundromat
- Start Maintenance Services
- Pool Cleaning Services
- Private Chef Service
- Shuttle/Driver Service
- Offer Airbnb Experiences
- Start an equipment hire business

These ventures aren't going to make you a millionaire, but they can add passive income to your bank account every month with very limited work after the initial set-up stage - especially if you're willing to hire staff for day-to-day operations.

Have a little fun with this. Play to your strengths and what you enjoy doing when you don't have to be doing something else (remember back to your brainstorming exercise). Make these extras fun tributaries that don't add a lot of stress to your plate and are something you enjoy working on.

Amazon Affiliate

This tributary is perfect for someone with moderate to advanced tech savvy who likes to be online - shopping, writing, posting, connecting with people. The only thing you need to set up an Amazon Affiliate program is a web site and an audience. Here's how it works and why you'd want to add this avenue of income into your pot.

Amazon is now one of the world's most famous and profitable online marketplaces, beating out big time box retailers like Walmart, Target, Sears, Kohl's, Best Buy, and Macy's combined. With a whopping valuation of over $356 BILLION, Amazon has changed the face of how we shop in the world today. While some of the smaller retailers are closing down shops across the globe, Amazon is growing at a steady pace.

As a small business owner, you can get on this bandwagon one of two ways-- as an **associate** or an **influencer**.

While it's a little bit easier to get in as an associate, the influencer program is easier for you to run. This is where you need to play to your strengths.

The Amazon Associate Program requires you to have a web site or a blog. You can do this very easily by setting up a free web site through a program like Wix. What would be on this web site? That depends on what you want to focus on.

The bottom line is you want to move products. You can easily tie this into your rental properties by setting up a simple website for each property that highlights items in the property that guests might use, enjoy, and want to order for themselves.

You will put a photo and description of each item on the web site, kind of like a catalog, and below that, you'll insert the Amazon affiliate link for ordering. When customers order through that link, you will get a percentage of sales.

The other option is the blog, but this can also be a page of your web site (which is what I'd recommend). Blogging about Airbnb hosting is a really popular topic right now, so that would be a great place to start. Then, once a week (or as often as you are able), choose a topic and write a post about it making sure to highlight one or more of the Amazon affiliate items so that you can link to it.

For example, one blog topic might be, "Airbnb Hosting at the Beach: Providing Outdoor Recreation."

This blog will talk about what kinds of outdoor recreation items to supply for your guests and what, if any, additional regulation and insurance that might require. In that blog post, you might talk about kayaks and boogie boards, frisbees, beach balls, beach bikes, and beach chairs. You would provide affiliate links to every one of those items on Amazon so that the people reading the blog post can order with just one click.

You can do this for all kinds of topics and categories, including bath and beauty, furniture and decor, kitchen products, snacks, coffee and coffee makers. The list goes on.

You can even do this without the step of setting up a website by just doing a blog. You can set up a blog simply and easily on Blogspot or Wordpress. But it seems that the affiliate program works best if your blog is linked to a website as well.

How To Set Up Your Amazon Associate Account

Now that you have your web site and/ or blog going, you're ready to set up your associate account.

1. Go to the Amazon Affiliate page at affiliate-program.amazon.com. It will look like this.

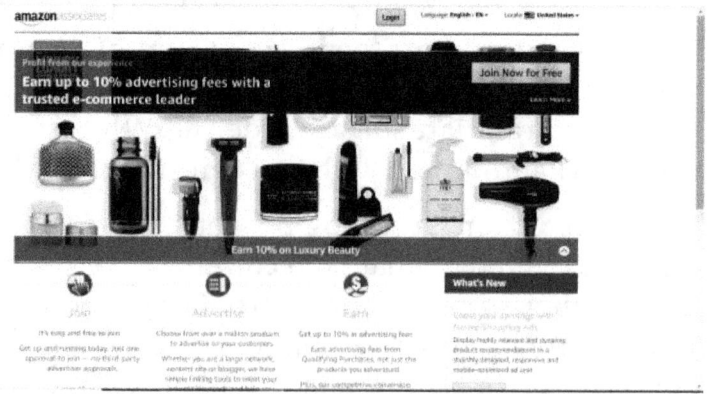

2. Click on "Join Now" at the bottom left hand side of the screen. The prompt will ask you to sign in to

your Amazon account. Next, you'll be asked to fill out your profile information and add your website link(s). They're going to want to check the site for content and traffic.
3. Next you'll be asked to complete your profile, which is about a one page questionnaire where you'll need to fill in the blanks.
4. Now they'll verify your identity by sending an automated phone call to the number you provide.
5. Tell them how you want to be paid. This is where you enter in all of your account information for payment collection!

You'll find out within a few days if you've been accepted into the program. Once you are accepted, you can access personal affiliate links for the products you want to promote, and you'll automatically be paid 1% - 10% of your verified product sales.

PRO TIP: Use Fiverr or Upwork to hire the writing and web site setup. Hire a web designer for a set budget and they will set up your website with all the required functionalities. Then, you can hire a regular blogger for a very small amount, and once given a list of topics they will post according to your schedule - and they will even insert your affiliate links. This makes your Amazon affiliate income completely passive.

Amazon Influencer Program

The Amazon Influencer Program is a newer program that's really starting to gain traction. While it's harder to get accepted into the program because of the program requirements, once you're in, it's easier to navigate and sell products.

The Influencer program counts on your social media presence on platforms like Instagram, YouTube, Twitter, and Facebook.

What is a social media influencer? A social media influencer is a user on a specific platform who has established credibility and a sizable following in a specific industry or niche. These influencers can use their authenticity and their reach to persuade followers...

And the influencers utilizing this program are seeing big returns-- anywhere from 10% commission on Amazon original branded merchandise like clothing, luggage and more, to 1% commision on video games and electronics.

So, that being said, the first thing you need to do is **set up and build up your social media accounts**. If your angle on this is "Airbnb Hosting" like in the affiliate program example, your best bet is to set up an Instagram, YouTube, Twitter (maybe not as good for this platform as the others), and/or Facebook account dedicated to nothing but hosting-related posts.

Here's a phenomenal example of an instagram account run by an Airbnb host:

FINANCIAL FREEDOM

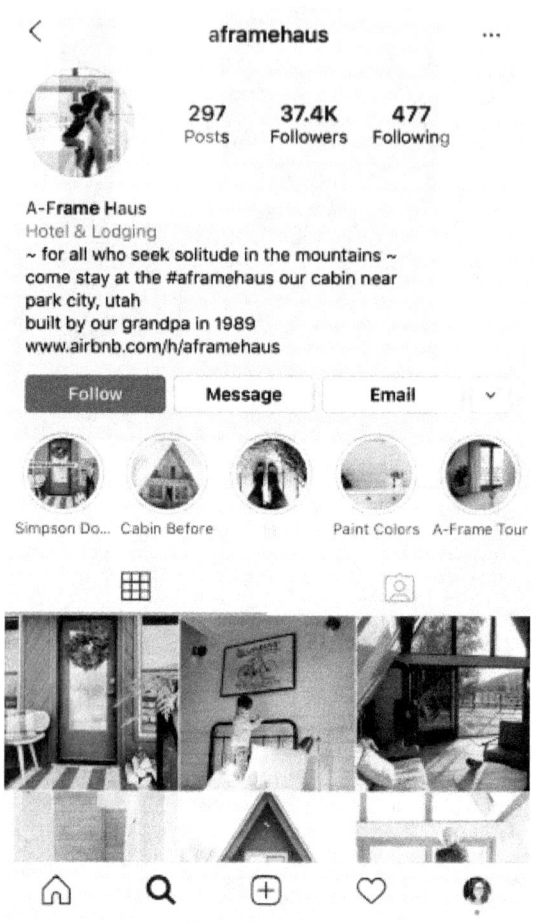

With 37.4K followers and beautifully photographed and nicely-captioned posts, this account would be a prime candidate for an Amazon Influencer account. How do you earn money from it, though?

Well, first of all, this social media is going to drive traffic to your Airbnb listing. That goes without saying.

Second, people will want what's in your posts.

Let's take a look at the photo on the left (of the sink). First of all, it's beautifully photographed, like everything else on this site. But not only that, it's also got a caption that tells a story and draws people in. It says,

"I chose this sink for one reason- It was the cutest (most convenient) tub for my baby boy. I think most mamas would agree with me."

And now if I'm a mama, and this captivating home and family has drawn me in, I want that tub… or at the very least I want that towel hanging over the edge or the wicker basket sitting beneath.

So, if this Instagrammer had an Amazon Influencer account, she'd have a link in her bio or on the post letting me know that's where I can purchase the items in the picture.

When I click on the link, it takes me to her Amazon storefront, where all of the items from her posts that can be purchased on Amazon are listed and categorized for easy shopping.

But it doesn't just have to be furniture and decor-- it could be the coffee you leave for guests, the organic laundry pods, or the granola bars you put in your hospitality basket. It could even be the keyless entry system - people buy everything on Amazon!

PRO TIP: Have your professional photographer photograph EVERYTHING when they come to take your staged photos for your listing. Even a close-up of the bag of coffee and mugs on the counter. This way, you can use these nice photos for your social media posts. So, make sure your space is staged with items you can purchase on Amazon (this works perfectly with your auto-order for disposables).

Items to consider for influencer links are: bath and beauty products, cleaning products, food and beverage, decor items like art prints and throw pillows, bedding, lock systems, video game systems, televisions, kitchen appliances, dishes and flatware, coffee table books, furniture, recreation items like kayaks and bicycles.

You're going to need to post on your account for quite some time, and spend time networking and building followers, before you apply for an influencer account. The good news is you can manage this account with minimal effort by **hiring a social media manager** who will take your photos and create the content for you. You can also create your own content and use a platform like Hootsuite to schedule out a month's worth of posts at a time.

And you don't need one account for each individual property. One to encompass all of your listings is fine, as long as it's done well.

Content creators are saying they're making a few dollars up to $1500 per month from their influencer storefronts.

Here's how to set up your Amazon Influencer account:

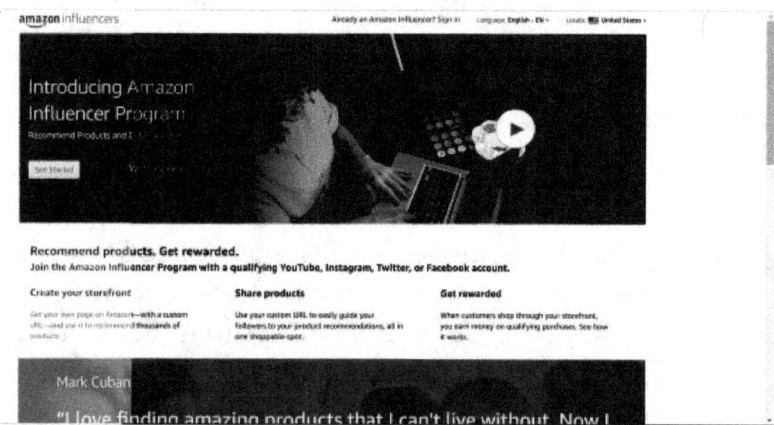

1. Go to the Amazon Influencer landing page: https://affiliate-program.amazon.com/influencers and click on "Get Started" tab. You'll be asked to link your Instagram, Facebook, YouTube, or Twitter accounts.
2. Get accepted. While Twitter and YouTube accounts are instantly vetted, it might take a few days for them to accept through your Facebook and Instagram. Be patient - and keep posting!

3. Set up a personal storefront with the custom URL you receive from Amazon. Fill your storefront with items you use in your properties and recommend to guests and followers.
4. Share the items and link to the custom URL so your followers can shop for your favorite things easily and conveniently on your page.
5. Start earning your commission!

The other way to use your Influener account is directly in your properties. When you purchase Amazon products for use in your rental properties, make sure you let your guests know!

You can do this by creating a shopping guide insert right inside your home manual, or simply by messaging the guests with a link to your Influencer storefront. A message might look like this:

> Hi Jane!
>
> I hope you're enjoying the complimentary Roos-Roast coffee! The "Lobster Butter" is our fave blend, and we've had a lot of guests ask where they can find it to brew at home.
>
> You can find the RoosRoast coffee and a lot of our other favorite items right here: [insert influencer store link]!
>
> Enjoy the coffee and have a great day.
>
> -Dean

Just a quick and simple message will get them to the page, and when they open it up, they'll see all of their favorite items in their stay right there in your storefront. They just have to click and the item will arrive at their home when they return.

Travel Guide

Who knows the area around your home better than you do? You've already dug your heels into the research before you rented your properties, and maybe you've also lived in the area for a long time. You know what the city, the neighborhood and the surrounding area has to offer.

What are the best night clubs, best beaches, favorite ice cream spots? Where is the best place to pick up a sandwich or buy a water raft?

Now, you can make that research serve double-duty and put it all in one convenient travel guide for digital or print.

Plus, now that you're not working a nine to five job, you have time to play tourist in your own city. Go take photos of the places you've been recommending but perhaps haven't had time to visit in a long time. See the city through the eyes of your potential guests.

Alternately, Google "license-free photos" or "open license photos" of the landmarks and use those to help create your travel guide. Beneath the photo, give a little review of each destination with the address, cost, and any other pertinent information a traveler to the area might need.

It is not difficult to put a book like this together and put it up for sale in digital format on Kindle or iBooks, or even print it and sell it to local venues to keep on hand for their customers..

And again, if you're not a writer or you need someone to edit and do the formatting, add a cover or do any of the graphic design, you can hire that out on Fiverr or Upwork.

Once the book is up for sale, you can refer your guests to it and your social media following as well. If it's on Amazon, you can add it to your influencer storefront. See how it all comes full circle?

Now, if you're spending your extra time traveling, like many Airbnb hosts do, you can absolutely do the same thing for the cities and countries you visit. Start your own separate Instagram for your travels and then link to your travel guides as well. Social media in this case is one of your best tools for advertising!

Give these guides a fun, unique, eye-catching title and keep the aesthetic of them uniform for brand recognition. Now, not only are you creating a nice additional income stream, your travels can come with a tax write-off because you are working!

Recreation Equipment Rental

Renting out recreational equipment like Jet Skis, kayaks, canoes, snowmobiles, and even bicycles or electric scooters, can be a really profitable business if you live in an area where those activities are popular.

Jet Ski Rental

If you're right on the water, weather it's a large recreational lake or the ocean, Jet skis are a popular vacation rental that can bring in a huge income - but you need to be prepared for a larger effort on startup and you'll have to put up some capital and the front end - that is, unless you already own a handful of jet skis for your family.

As a vacation rental host, you're already in the tourism business, especially if your location is in a tourist destination. And if this destination is on the water, you should consider the Jet Ski rental business.

A rental business is a lucrative start-up for an ambitious entrepreneur, and it especially links well to your oceanside/ lakeside rental property because you have a built-in captive target market.

The Jet Ski rental business caters to vacationers wanting to have the thrill and excitement of riding the waves on their personal water-motorcycle. This kind of business makes a profit by renting out jet skis by the hour or the day to customers over the age of sixteen (and requires a valid form of ID).

Before you get started, first check your location to make sure that a recreational rental is allowed. You can do this by calling the city offices or even the chamber of commerce. OR, you can walk down to the beach and if there are other rental businesses, you can bet it's allowed. (But do call to make sure.)

About the Industry

If you're on a coastal location that attracts fun-loving people who want to venture into watersports, your jet ski business can be lucrative… as long as you know a bit about the maintenance and operation of a jet ski - or (here's the key) you can hire someone who does.

Challenges that you'll have to overcome starting your jet ski rental are 1, obtaining the business license, 2, getting the right location (or the off-site option which we'll discuss below), 3, keeping costs down.

Let's start with number three - cost. We all want to know how much it's going to cost us to start a new venture before we invest too much time and energy into it. And, unless you already have your own Jet skis, the cost of this venture can be high.

New jet skis can range in price from $2500 - $10,000 depending on brand and model, but you can get used jet skis for about half of that price. You will need to consider your budget, and rely on market research to understand your demand.

For example, if you're located on a small recreational inland lake, you may only need four or five Jet Skis to meet market demand. If you're on a very busy beach that's packed with partying college students at spring break, you may want to consider a fleet of ten jet skis.

Market Analysis

Who are you catering your jet ski business to?

Well, the good news is that you've already done this research when you were thinking about who you're marketing your rental property to! It would be the same type of clientele if you're opening this business either on the same property or in the same location as your rental unit.

Plus, you know the traffic in the area. Is it busy year-round, or mostly during the summer/spring/winter? Is it mostly families, or mostly millennials, or is it baby boomers taking their second honeymoon?

By understanding your target market, you'll know what types of packages to offer with your rental business.

You'll have to decide if you want to offer group rates, day rates, or keep it by the hour. Can a group reserve the jet skis ahead, or is it first-come first-serve?

Now, you understand who you're selling this service to, it's also important to understand who you're competing with. Go scope out the other rental services near you.

What are their prices? How busy are they? How many jet skis do they have? What kinds of packages do they offer?

Now you need to think about how you're going to compete.

Are you able to offer something that they are not offering? Maybe a group rate or a guided tour of the area on jet ski?

Business Model and Startup Options

The most time-intensive and cost-intensive is to **start from scratch** with a location on the beach. You will need to:

- Buy or rent the property (unless this is on your own beachfront)
- Make sure it's zoned for the business prior to doing so
- Get your business license
- Get your business insurance/ set up an LLC
- Purchase and set up your building/ trailer/ storage
- Get signage and marketing materials made
- Purchase your Jet Skis and safety equipment
- Hire a manager/ staff

As you can see, this setup process is not super complicated, but it's not a no-effort kind of thing. The second option is a bit simpler - purchase an existing franchise.

Purchase a Franchise

There are four really good jet ski franchise opportunities with various benefits:

Jetski Safari

With over 12 years of operating experience in the jet ski rental business, jet ski Safari is considered the industry gold standard when it comes to jet ski and ocean adventures.

Jet ski Safari offers its user a complete sea-sport experience, and stands behind it's franchisees with its knowledge, support, and services.

Most Jet Ski rentals are sole proprietorships or small business LLC's. Jetski Safari offers it franchisees corporate backup, troubleshooting, and product stability. From HR trouble to mechanical issues, this comp;any's corporate office is there to help you as an owner. This helps take some of the anxiety out of starting your own rental business.

Franchise Fee

Jet Ski Safari is offering to waive any franchise fees or royalties for their first 100 franchisees.

Jet Ski Safari offers the following support to its franchise owners: A large well-stocked spare parts inventory, 24 hours support line, a constant stream of booking (so no idle jet skis = more money), 3 jet ski types for 3 different operations, cheaper spare parts and lower operation costs.

Trax Powersports Rentals

Renting from TRAX PowerSports Rentals® is a full service watersports company that goes beyond just jet skis. TRAX PowerSports Rentals® provides you with: Boat Rentals, Personal Watercraft/Jet-Ski Rentals, jet skis, wakeboards, surfboards, tubes, and all the accessories.

TRAX Powersports Rentals is dedicated to helping its franchisees fulfill their vision for their rental business. Owning a TRAX PowerSports Rentals Franchise will seamlessly fit with your home rental business and provide a steady additional income stream.

Trax provides you with access to their proven systems, policies, and procedures that promote efficiency and profitability, as well as ongoing training, support and development, and brand promotion and marketing materials.

Franchise Fees

- Franchise Fee – $39,000
- Franchise Royalty – 6% on Gross Monthly Rentals
- National Ad Fund – 2% of Gross Monthly Rentals

Invert Sports

Invert Sports is an 18 year old company that has been providing quality service to its recreational equipment clients across the U.S. This full service water and outdoor sports company supplies boats, jet skis, ATV, snowmobiles, water sport instruction, and private recreational tours of all types.

Invert Sports has a reputation of being one of the best equipment providers in the industry, covering 3,000 lakes across the country and offering all kinds of charter services for various niches - family, friends, corporate team-building adventures.

The company offers franchises and provides incredible assistance to their franchisees, including evaluating location opportunities prior to purchase to determine what type of business model to use and what scale of operation would best suit them. They also provide the franchisee with an established and trusted brand, a protected territory, extensive custom training for your staff, fleet purchase discounts, complete operations support, and marketing materials.

Franchise cost

- Liquid Assets to purchase equipment: $120,000 – $300,000
- Investment Cost for Consultation or Contract Territory Fee: $35,000
- Ongoing Contract Fee: 8% of gross revenue

As you can see, startup costs for your business, even with a franchise, can be considerable. Here's another option to make a little bit of extra income stream without the major investment of time and capital.

Jet Ski Concierge

For lack of a better term, I call this the jet ski concierge. For this business all you need is a couple of jet skis, a trailer, a place to store the jet skis, and a friend. Okay... they don't have to be a friend, just someone willing to help move the jet skis or hook up a trailer.

For your own personal protection, you likely want to also get a license for the business, insurance, and an LLC... all very easy to obtain.

And you can start this in a number of ways-- first, **take stock of your assets**.

- Do you have jet skis and a trailer?
- Do you have an unused garage or storage shed?
- Do you have a friend with a truck and hitch wanting to make some extra money?
- Is there public beach access for boat launching near you?
- Do you own beachfront property?
- Do you have any financial capital?

What you already have will determine what your next step is. But to get this small jet ski rental started, all you really need to do is have the Jet skis and the trailer along with the life jackets. Get your rental license and insurance. Set it up so that whenever someone wants to rent/share your jet skis, they reserve through the concierge (the friend who will take care of the rental). The guest can pay through PayPal or Venmo, show the payment to the concierge, and the concierge can either open up the storage and help the guest hook up the trailer or meet the guest at the designated launch site (for an extra fee).

Make sure you have the guest read and sign a safety procedure document and insurance waiver. You can find templates for both of those online with a quick search.

Now, advertise this through your listing, in the guest book that you provide about things to do locally, and you can even reach beyond the scope of your guests to advertise this online and in local papers.

This model works best for all-day rentals, not one hour rentals. That is, unless your concierge is willing to sit at the beach and make the exchanges.

Kayak/ Canoe/ Paddle Board Rentals

If your properties are on or near a river, creek, lake, pond, beach, or other body of water, kayak, canoe, and paddle board rentals are a super popular business! And it's a lot cheaper and easier startup than a jet ski business.

First, decide what caliber kayak business you want to start and gage accordingly. As the same questions you asked when you started your home rental, and the same kinds of questions as stated in the jet ski section.

What are your goals? What are your assets?

The great thing about a non-motorized rental business is that you do not need indoor storage for the crafts. You just need a place outdoors to store them safely from theft (you can lock them with one long chain and lock), a place to hang and store your lifejackets and paddles, and a place to launch.

Your kayak rental business can consist of you renting out a couple of kayaks on the river to a full-service rental with guided tours and lessons complete with shuttle service. Decide what type of business you want to operate.

FINANCIAL FREEDOM

The best case scenario is that you own waterfront property and can operate your business right from your own beachfront/riverfront.

If that's not the case, the next best thing is to partner with an existing waterfront/riverfront business.

Is there a bar, marina, restaurants, ice cream shack, beach umbrella rental, or other business in the area you're targeting that would be willing to partner with you for use of space (and even staff-sharing, potentially)?

One you find your location, it's time to work with your city/municipality to make sure you're doing everything according to code. A kayak or canoe rental business can be risky, so work with existing community organizations or reach out to currently-operating partnerships in the community for assistance.

It definitely works best to start your kayak rental business with an existing waterfront business or a municipality, or a currently-running organization. Why try to shove open the door when you could hold hands with someone who already has their foot in?

It's best if your location has the following amenities:
- Restrooms
- Running water
- Storage (for life preservers, paddles, and anything that cannot be safely locked with a chain)

Purchasing your watercraft: New kayaks can run anywhere from $200 each to $2,000 each. But the good news is that, for your business, I recommend getting the less-expensive models and to *buy used!*

You can always find kayaks on Craigslist and Facebook Marketplace, and some are as low as $75.

But let's say you purchase new (so they all match). You can get the $200 - $250 model WITH paddle at Costco, Walmart, and off-season you can find that deal at big watersports outfitters. Make sure that you're purchasing a range of sizes and paddle-lengths.

Paddle boards can be purchased for anywhere between $300 for a lower model board to $3,000 for a competition board. The same goes for the paddle boards - buy used or get the cheaper models from the big box stores.

Canoes are a bit more expensive, but they are a two-person craft and so you will rent them out at a slightly higher rate. A low-end canoe will cost about $500-$600 and then they can go all the way up into the thousands. Having said that, you can often find used canoes for sale in local papers and in the same online resale platforms.

Permits, Certifications, and Insurance: Non-motorized boats typically do not require a state license unless you plan to use public Fish & Boat launches. Cost per boat is approximately $10 per year.

Do you want to have a variety or specialize in just one type of craft? Determine the size and makeup of your fleet and buy accordingly.

Don't forget, you will also need a range of life preservers - small youth to adult XL. Life jackets typically run about $35 - $55 each.

AND paddles! Canoe paddles are their own separate breed from the other two crafts. Kayaks have a double-bladed paddle and paddle boards have their own paddle as well. Remember to get a variety of lengths to meet the needs of all of your customers.

Staff: You will need to hire a staff to run your operation. It's important that this staff should have at a minimum, First Aid and CPR certification. Other additional certifications that are good to have would be the Boater Safety Course and a Water

Rescue Certification.

Insurance: You absolutely must consult with your insurance agent, making sure they are familiar with water rental operations. You want to be adequately protected not only against damage, but also for liability.

Waivers: Put together a customer waiver to sign releasing you of any liability in the case of any personal or bodily harm, loss of property or property damage, et cetera. You can easily find a template for this online.

Setting up your Business

To get your business started, you want to register with the IRS to receive an Employe Identification Number (EIN). Once you have the EIN, you can open a bank account in the business name.

Next, secure a Sales Tax license from the municipality out of which you plan to operate. For any new business, resources can be made available through your local Small Business Development Center or Chamber of Commerce.

Once you find your location and set up, you'll need to hire and train staff. The size of your staff can range from one person to many depending on the scope of your business.

The startup of any kind of rental business is pretty extensive. This is not an avenue of passive income that you want to create if you do not have the tie or enthusiasm to get it off the ground. But with the right staff in place, and a busy watersport location, your rental business could bring in a tidy income.

Bicycle Rental

If your properties are in an area that is difficult to get around in by car (for example, if it is high traffic and/ or if it has difficult parking or expensive parking), or if you're in an area that's fun and touristy to bicycle (like the beach), you might want to consider adding a bike rental service to your repertoire and another income stream.

Do you remember when you'd find a pile of bicycles outside the comic shop, ice cream shop, or the movie theatre on a Saturday afternoon? There would be a slew of bikes at the beach or lining the fences at the baseball diamond...

In tourist towns like Northern Michigan's Mackinac Island or the sunny beaches of southern Florida, you'll still see cyclings tooling around town. And you'll definitely see the ten-speeds lining the streets and highways - these are the sports cyclists (which are a different breed entirely).

Despite the coming of the self-driving car and the strange zooming of the hoverboards... the future is not yet here, and there is still a need and the desire for good old fashioned peddling.

This is where you come in - you're starting a bike rental business!

The process is simple - you take a fee for a half or full day rental (or you can rent hourly in high-demand areas). The clients put down a deposit (that is returned when the bike is returned), pay the fee, sign a waiver, and they ride off on a bike!

Start-Up Costs: Your primary startup cost is for your fleet of bicycles. You want to consider varied styles and sizes of bikes, including bicycles for children, tandem bikes, and wide-seated bicycles for the older clientele. You must also purchase the same number of helmets, or more, in order to offer your clients size choices to fit various sized heads!

In addition to the equipment, you'll need money for bike repairs, staff, and a location to store the bicycles. For the location, it's preferable that you partner with an existing business that has high tourist or walking traffic, or that you use your own property if it's in a high exposure area.

Finally, you will need to pay for insurance, both liability and property damage, for your business as well as an LLC if you're not putting this business underneath the umbrella of another.

Start-Up Cost: $5,000–$9,000

This estimate is based on a fleet of 10 - 20 new bicycles with helmets. The bicycles will run you approximately $300 each, but this could go up or down depending on the type and brand of cycle you're wanting to offer. Choose inexpensive though solid ones. $300/unit is a correct budget.

This also includes hiring someone to run the rental business for the first four weeks. However, you should start seeing a substantial income in a high traffic area in the first week.

Typical Fees: $20 - $30 per ½ day rental

Potential Earnings: $5,000 - $30,000 (varies greatly)

Obviously, the earning potential is going to be based primarily on location and competition. If you're the only (or one of just a few) bike rental(s) at a beach resort location that does not lend well to driving traffic, you're looking at a super lucrative business!

Laundromat

When you run a R2R business with 40 or 50 properties, you will realize how much you spend per month to have a quality washing and ironing of your linens, blankets, covers and towels. Thousands and thousands of Dollars every month. You will start to think that opening your own Laundry Shop would not be such a bad idea, as you will start with one big client already-- Your own self.

A coin laundry can be a really lucrative business, especially in urban areas and areas with quite a few apartment buildings. However, the startup for a coin laundry can be high. You're looking at approximately $200,000 - $500,000 for a moderate sized (2,000 sq feet) business in a well-trafficked area. This is the cost to purchase an existing business (which I would recommend).

The startup for a new laundry business is not only higher but more involved. You can anticipate approximately $200,000 just to renovate your 2,000 square foot space (which you have to lease or purchase), and then the bulk of the remaining expense will be for equipment. And then there are the licensing fees, including:

- Business license
- Health department
- Impact Fees
- Signage Permit
- Fire Department permit
- Air and Water Pollution Control Permit

Of course, these fees will vary per municipality, so you'll have to check with your local government agency to get a more accurate idea. Then there are some "hidden" costs to be aware of, including a municipal sewer connection fee which can range anywhere from $200 - $8,000 per washing machine. (For an average sized laundromat, you'll want approximately 25 - 30 machines.)

You can avoid these fees by purchasing an existing business!

Now, the fantastic thing about coin laundry is that it is a largely automated business. You can even leave it open 24 hours, especially in busy urban areas. You set up the machines, set up a coin/change machine (alternately, you can card-reader machines) and a vending machine service for laundry soaps and dryer sheets.

FINANCIAL FREEDOM

Once this is all in place (or you have purchased it complete), you just need to hire someone to come in once per day to clean and check on the machines. The vending machines come with their own services that refill on a regular basis, so you don't need to worry about those.

Finally, and you may wish to do this yourself or hire a very trusted senior employee, you need someone to empty the coins, record the daily income, and deposit the money. I suggest hiring a "manager" that would do this as well as take care of any bill payments, ordering, dealing with maintenance issues, and et cetera.

This way your coin laundry business is fully automated, and can generate you up to around $350,000 per year for a busy, well-maintained operation.

Maintenance Services

We have mentioned many times how important it is for the Rent to Rent business to have a precise, high level and especially fast maintenance service. So why not hire your own team and offer the services also to other clients to maximise the profits?

There are a lot of handymen and women out there who are excellent at their work, but not interested in running their own business. This is where you come in. You provide the business platform, the marketing, and you take care of all the licensing and insurance, money collection, taxes, et cetera, and they provide the maintenance.

The first thing you will need to do is check the laws in your state for **licensing requirements** for the various skills you are going to offer: plumbing, electric, contractor's, those are the primary three. The best thing would be to look for contractors who are already licensed in their respective areas.

Now, you will want to set up an LLC (Limited Liability Corporation), for your maintenance business. This will help protect you and your other assets in the case of a lawsuit.

Now, choose a logo design to go with your business name, set up a phone line and a web site, create business cards, and hire your employees! You can decide if you want to hire them as actual employees or as independent contractors paid per job.

To create a brand loyalty and recognition, it would be great to provide Logo shirts for all of your employees, and perhaps even Logo stickers for their vehicles (which will provide instant advertising).

Some of the best advertising to do for this business in addition to the vehicle stickers is targeted Facebook ads. These ads are inexpensive and allow you to target a certain demographic and region.

Pool Cleaning Services

Pool cleaning services are obviously something you'd most likely use and therefore offer in warm climate areas where pools are prevalent, and it would work in a similar way to starting the handyman service.

Create your business name, logo, and form and LLC. With this one, however, you may want to consider purchasing your own equipment and perhaps a vehicle, and then hire one or two pool cleaners (or more depending on scale) to staff your business.

The good news is that starting a pool cleaning business is relatively inexpensive. YOu can get going for about $2,000 investment - and the pool cleaning business is a $3 billion industry.

Your $2,000 investment includes water test kits, skimmers, brushes, and leaf rakes. You will also need a vehicle large enough to transport the equipment, such as a van or a truck.

You can get around this cost by hiring pool cleaners who supply their own vehicle, offering to pay them mileage while on the job.

Get t-shirts made for your staff and even a car logo magnetic decal - as both are cheap and easy advertising and help build brand recognition.

Before you get started advertising (again, Facebook targeted ads are a good idea), make sure you pull all the proper permits and licenses for your municipality and it's always best to have insurance!

According to HomeAdvisor, a pool service average cost is:
- $177 for weekly services
- $267 for bi-weekly services
- $190 for monthly services
- $266 for opening and closing only

A pool service owner makes approximately $50-$60 per hour. So, if you pay your staff person $20 - $25 per hour, you are making a tidy profit!

Private Chef Service

A private chef service is a fantastic pairing with a vacation rental property, especially if you're catering to high end guests, although not only... You will be surprised to see how many renting a simple condo from you would like to have a private chef service at home at least one evening! You can offer this service right inside of your guest book, or even include it in your listing description.

You may be surprised at the cost of a private chef, but trust me, your wealthier guests are not. The average rate for a private chef are as follows:
- $75 - $125 and up per person for one meal. This is all-inclusive and could vary by menu. The chef will shop for

the meal, cook (often bringing their own knives and utensils), serve, and clean up afterward. This cost is typically for a three or four-course meal. For a meal with wine-pairing offered by a classically trained chef, the cost could reach $250 per person.

- $500 - $600 per day for a day rate, plus food. This would be for someone who prefers to have the chef on hand cooking all of the meals for the day. Typically this would cover two meals a day plus a cocktail hour.
- $2500 - $3500 per week (6 day week), plus food. This option would likely be utilized by a celebrity guest, or a very wealthy guest, anyway. This would cover the two meals per day plus cocktail hour.

To get this started, all you really need to do is contact several chefs in your area, or put an advertisement out. Ask if they would be interested in being connected to clients that are renting out your property. After thoroughly vetting your chefs, make sure that they agree that you will be taking 20% commission on their fee (or whatever is agreed-upon).

Or even better... My advice. Hire a young talented chef. Offer him a fixed salary + commissions. That would be a great deal for both and will keep your fixed expenses at minimum and his/her earning potential and motivation high. You can test the market with freelancers and then, when you have good response and enough market information, just go with your own staff.

It's important here that you figure out liability insurance. If your chef does not carry his/her own, it could be best to open an LLC for this purpose and take out your own liability insurance, and then pay your chefs through the LLC.

This business can be incredibly lucrative, again especially if you are in the luxury rental market, and it requires very little effort on your part once it is established.

Shuttle/ Driver Service Or Uber/Lyft Service

A shuttle or driver service pairs well with a rental property business, especially if you own multiple properties in one area. Having said that, the licensing for such a business can be difficult to obtain and costly, depending on where your business is located. So, before you pursue this route any further, check into the license fees in your area. (Or even much easier, make it an Uber or Lyft vehicle - which is a simple registration process on the respective app.)

If you decide that it's doable, the first thing you need to do (after you obtain your license, LLC, and insurance) is obtain (lease) a vehicle. Make sure your vehicle meets the needs of the target market. For example, if your properties are geared toward families, you may want to get a van or a larger SUV. If you specialize in luxury vacation homes, maybe a town car is better suited.

Now, it's time to hire your driver. Your driver could even be your Property Manager at the beginning, if you have hired one. What's better than optimizing costs and time? Or it could even be yourself if it's your first property and this business is not yet running for you as Passive Income Stream.

Your driver is going to be the face of your business (and will pretty much run it for you), so make sure you vet him or her carefully. You will be hiring someone who already has a chauffeur's license, giving them the proper authority to drive your commercial vehicle.

Once you hire your driver, make sure you set them up to take payment via credit card. You can do this easily with a Square- an app with a small square attachment for their phone which they swipe. OR, you can require that all payments be made up front using whatever advance payment platform you set up for your business (Stripe, PayPal, Venmo, etc). Or add the cost directly on top of the Airbnb or Vrbo booking cost (if the shuttle service is for your guests).

It would also benefit you to set up a simple web site - you can do this for free or a nominal monthly fee on Shopify (my favourite solution) or Wix.com (very simple to use), or hire someone through Fiverr to do it for you. This way you can set up payment directly on the web site, and you can start to offer this service to other clients as well different from your properties' guests. Have your driver check the site and make sure that he/she does the pickups according to schedule.

For this business, you pay the driver a set percentage per ride and you take the rest to pay your expenses and then a profit. Or at a certain point, once again, you can directly hire one on a permanent basis and full time.

This can be an excellent extra service to offer your guests (airport pickup is fantastic), and the driver can schedule additional rides when they are not busy with your guests - thus generating more income!

Offer Airbnb Experiences

Airbnb experiences are a fantastic way to make extra income - especially if you are personally involved! I know, this means it's not a passive income... but usually an Airbnb Experience is offered by a host who has a passion for something and wants to share it with their guests, or even just travelers who are interested and book.

As an Airbnb Experience host, you offer a deeper, more meaningful experience for your guests than a touristy activity would offer. For example, you might offer a personal wine country tour in your convertible classic car followed by a tasting with appetizers in your private garden. You'd offer this because it doesn't feel like work to you - because doing this is fun (while also profitable). This could be priced however you see fit - but somewhere in the ballpark of $300 per couple for the afternoon experience sounds about right.

Airbnb Experiences have a broad range - all the way from walking with wolves in a rescue sanctuary ($180 per person), to painting walls with a street artist in Barcelona ($146 per person), and everything in between.

An Experience could even be taking a group on a pub crawl of your favorite local places wherein you include a set menu plus one drink per pub per person! You are only limited by your creativity and passion.

Plus, the great thing about the Airbnb Experience is that you set your calendar so you are only available to book when you want to be.

If you want a perfectly-paired extra income stream to your rental business that requires very little effort- and the effort you do put in is fun - this is the one for you. All you have to do is decide what experience you want to offer and set it up through Airbnb.

Start An Equipment Hire Business

An equipment hire business rents out everything from strollers and deluxe air beds to tents and DJ equipment. The great thing about this type of business is that you can go with a niche or you can go big from the get-go. You just need to figure out what you want to do based on your desires, your storage and transport capabilities, and your budget.

If you want to stay smaller, requiring just a small storage space (either at a storage unit or in an owned garage), you could focus on renting out these types of items:

- Strollers (single and double)
- Pack and plays / cribs
- Deluxe air beds with full linens

- Wheelchairs
- Power scooters
- Gaming Systems (Xbox, Playstation)
- Car seats and booster chairs
- High chairs
- Collapsible ping-pong table
- Carpet and upholstery steamers
- Espresso/cappuccino machine
- Folding plastic buffet/card tables
- Folding chairs
- Movie projectors

If you have a large space and the moving capability (i.e. box truck or van), you can rent out larger, more expensive items like:

- Party tents (plus tables and chairs)
- Full wedding service (tents/tables/chairs/covers/dishes)
- Sound and lighting equipment
- Photobooths
- Portable dance floors
- DJ equipment and sound system
- Portable bars
- Outdoor refrigerators
- Popcorn machines
- Gym equipment (treadmill/ exercise bike/ weights)
- Massage beds
- Bounce houses
- Camping tents
- Kayaks

The primary cost of this business is the purchase of the equipment you plan to rent. Once that is determined, you will need to store the equipment (again, you either own a garage or you rent a space in a storage facility).

Remember, before you get too far, set up your LLC and get your insurance!

Now, you have to hire staff to deliver and/or set up the equipment when it is rented out, and then pick it up or/and disassemble. The staff will also be responsible for maintaining the equipment as needed.

Once you purchase your equipment, photograph the equipment and set up your web site. You can either do this yourself using a platform like Shopify, or you can hire someone on Fiverr to do this for you. It's best if you can take payment right on your web site.

Once it's all set up, you can advertise to your airbnb guests and also to the local community. Utilize Facebook and Instagram targeted advertising, SEO keywords on your web site, Google ADS, and you can also take out ads in your area's local paper and shopping guides.

Your startup costs and your income potential for this business are going to vary widely based on what type of equipment you offer. You're really only limited by your imagination - and what the market is looking for!

Local Guide Ad Sales

The guests staying with you love to have tips and insight into the area, and to be able to access restaurants and local attractions quickly and easily.

The local guide is different than a travel guide. This is more like a local yellow pages for anything your guest would want or need while they're at your rental.

Start by breaking the guide into different categories. Some suggestions for categories are:
- Dining
  - Breakfast
  - Lunch

- Dinner
- Cocktails/lounge
- Live music
- Family Friendly
- Vegetarian/Vegan
- Allergen friendly
- Delivery
- Attractions
    - Outdoor attractions
    - Movie theatres
    - Live theatre
    - Educational
    - Shopping centers
    - Outdoor recreation/ water sports
    - Concert venue
- Transportation
    - Lyft / Uber
    - Taxi/ Metro Car
    - Bus Station
    - Train Station
    - Airport
    - Trolly
    - Bike/ Scooter rental
    - Car rental
- Medical
    - Emergency Room/ Hospital
    - Urgent Care Clinic
    - Veterinarian
- Gifts/ Flowers
- Beauty/Hair/Spa
- Grocery/ Health Food Store
- Large Retail Chains
- Bakeries and Sweets
- Pet Boarding / Grooming

Now, list as many retailers as possible under each category.

Once you have them listed, write a short description along with a phone number, address, and website (if possible).

If you feel inspired and you have the capability, you can also add a photo of the business to the listing.

I'm sure you're wondering at this point how you are going to make money by providing this service to your guests! This is where some legwork comes in on your part.

Approach as many of the businesses as possible asking them if they'd like to purchase ad space in your travel book. Let them know how many guests come through your listing (or listings if you have multiple locations in the same city) per month, per year.

Allow them to purchase a business card sized, quarter, half, or full page ad that can include a coupon if they desire. Explain that the ad will run until the book is updated (decide the duration - maybe it's quarterly). At this point, they can renew the ad if they are seeing results.

Make sure you keep a record of who and how you contacted the business to make renewal followup easy.

Rate Suggestions:

Full Page Ad - $150

½ Page Ad - $75

¼ Page Ad - $40

Business Card Ad - $20

You can put all the ads in one section at the back of the book, or I suggest putting the ads in the sections that are relevant to the business.

Now, add a creative cover to your guide booklet. Once you get your booklet completely put together, simply using Microsoft Word, Google Docs, or some other program, you can print it at any UPS Store, FedEx Store, or other print shop for relatively cheap. Print in color on heavy glossy stock if possible. This way you prevent tearing and the need for reprinting.

Keep a dozen or so of these in the cleaning closet and have your cleaning service leave a copy of this booklet on the counter near the welcome basket.

Small Business Agreements

Everyone has a friend that's part of a multi-level marketing scheme. I know, we're taught to run far away from the "pyramid," but some of these businesses actually sell fantastic and useful products that could be really marketable to your guests.

For example, Melaleuca markets tea tree oil, but they also sell really good all natural household cleaners, body products, and first aid products. PartyLite has wonderful scented candles and stylish candle holders that could compliment your decor. Young Living and dOTERRA sell essential oils that can be diffused to make your home smell good (and, as they claim, alleviate stress or relieve your headache).

What I propose is that you contact the local representative from those multi-level marketing companies, and other MLM companies like this, and offer that team member an opportunity.

Trust me, these sales people are always ready and willing to jump on a new opportunity.

Here's what they give you: They put their product in your rental unit, or units, and they can put their information on a sticker on the bottle or it can be printed in your home guide or posted on the wall in the appropriate room. This way, when a guest falls in love with the scent of Eucalyptus being diffused in the master bedroom, they can order.

FINANCIAL FREEDOM

The representative gives you free product to have in your property, and a percent of his or her commission from every sale or the new subscription generated by you and your guests.

Here's what you're offering them: First hand intimate exposure of their product to potential customers with real-life usage. When your guest washes their hair in the brand's luxurious lavender-mint shampoo, they're going to want to buy it for themselves. No selling for you (the team member) do to - the product speaks for itself.

Here's a list of MLM companies that might be useful products to have in your properties:

Melaleuca

All natural bath and beauty products, household cleaners, first aid products, feminine and personal hygiene products, vitamins and supplements and some fitness foods.

Other MLM companies that offer similar products are: Arbonne International, Forever Living, Nature's Sunshine Products, Shaklee International

Beach Body

Leave a set of the Beach Body BlueRay DVD's next to your BlueRay player to give your guests a free workout with a personal trainer! Most of these workouts require no special equipment and many do not even require shoes. Of course, the rep gives you the DVD's and a commission on any sales they earn from your guests.

Discovery Toys

ENGINEERING LITTLE MINDS

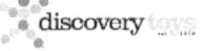

This company offers a wide range of educational toys for kids of all ages. These would be fantastic to have in your home if you have a family-friendly rental. The rep would give you the toys and make sure there is a sticker on them letting guests know where to purchase - you get a commission from any sales generated!

Pampered Chef

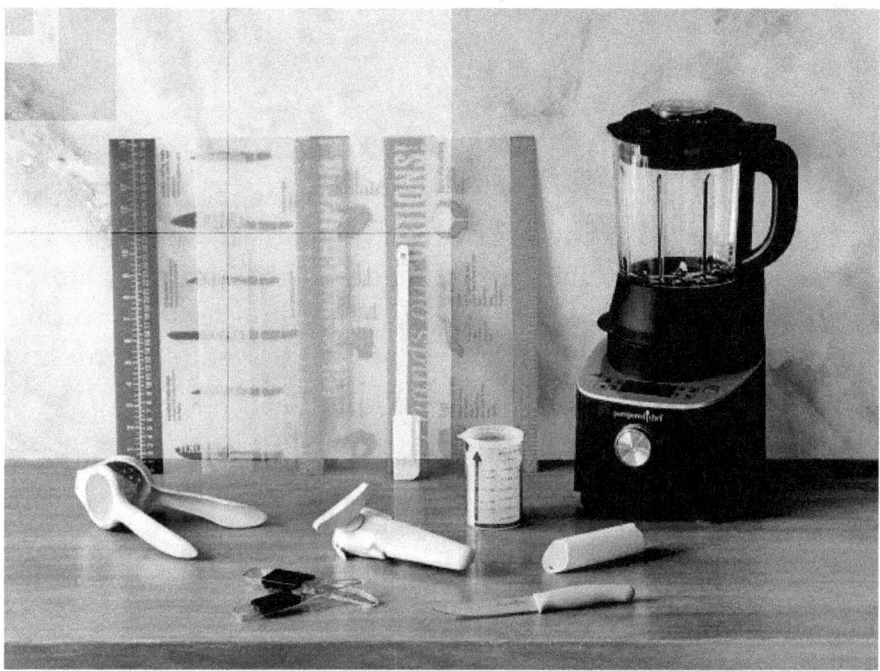

Pampered Chef offers a huge collection of kitchen items including everything from pots and pans to handy kitchen gadgets like can openers and garlic presses, perfect to stock your rental's full kitchen… or even one or two of their microwave pots would be great for an efficient kitchen! Best part is they provide your kitchen supplies and you get a commission from any orders generated.

PartyLite

PartyLite is a home styling candle and decor company that has recently also expanded into scented oils and wax burners. These kinds of touches can turn your rental unit up a notch and make it feel more like home. When guests want to take home the scent of their lovely vacation, you get a commission and/or free product from the PartyLite rep!

doTerra

FINANCIAL FREEDOM

An oil diffuser is a great, safe way to make your property smell fresh and homey. Lighten up the scent in the bathroom or give your kitchen a warm, sugary aroma with diffused essential oils from a company like doTERRA.

Other companies that sell similar items: Young Living, BeYoung, SimplyAroma, TruVision Health, Zija International, NYR Organic, Scentsy

You can also do something similar **with local businesses.**

Talk to the local bakery about providing muffins or bagels, or something more shelf stable like packaged biscotti. Is there a local winery or brewery? They might like your property to feature their wine or a growler of their microbrew or cider. Local chocolatier or candy shop? Perfect little treat for your welcome basket.

The list can go on: Interior designers or home decor stores can provide furnishing and decor, local artists can put artwork on your walls, the coffee shop and roaster up the block might want your guests to sample their single pot coffee pack!

Make sure the number or web site is listed on the label for guests to order more! The company you're partnering with gains a customer and a sale, and perhaps even a subscriber or a new team member. You gain a little bit of passive income and free product for your property.

It's a win-win situation.

Car-Sharing

Car-sharing income is something I discussed in my last book, but it's definitely worth a mention here, as well. Why? Because how convenient would it be for your guests if they can rent your car when they rent your condo?

Turo is a site that allows you to rent out your car short-term similar to renting out your apartment on Airbnb! The service will cost users somewhere between $25 and $185 per day, and that provides you with a tidy income.

Turo gives its car-loaners up to $1 Million in insurance which includes roadside assistance, giving you and your clients a sense of security that they and your vehicle will be safe.

The average Turo user, lending out one car, earns around $500 per month. But, that doesn't take into consideration the built-in market you'd have with direct advertising in your rental property guest list.

You can get started making money with Turo in several different ways. One, you can list your own car when you're not using it and instead share a car with your spouse/ partner or take public transit.

Two, you can purchase vehicles specifically for Turo-sharing. If you are using this approach, make sure you study your market carefully to ensure that you'll get back your initial and monthly investment.

Consider the cost of the vehicle, monthly payment, upkeep, and insurance.

Having said that, if you have a completely booked out rental unit in an area where guests typically need a vehicle to get around, you could potentially make a killing on your vehicle.

Let's look at the numbers: You utilize some of your rental property revenue and pay outright for a $6,000 excellent condition used mid class SUV. Your rental property is in Austin, Texas.

Insurance on your new car is about $150 per month. You're able to rent out your new "extra car" for about $50 per day, 23 days out of the month. That's a net per month of $1,000. In six months your car is paid off and **you're bringing in $1,000 per month in passive income**.

Reinvesting Your Capital

Now that you have your successful rent-to-rent business and it's generating a tidy income, plus your smaller passive income tributaries, what do you do with all of this "extra money?"

Well... generate another income stream, what else?

And the most passive way to stream income is to put your money somewhere and let it grow. But where should you put your money?

There are a number of good answers to this, depending on a number of factors, including: Certificates of Deposit, Treasury Securities, Government Bond Funds, Municipal Bond Funds, Short-term Corporate Bond Funds, Dividend-paying stocks, High Yield savings Accounts, Growth Stocks, Growth Stock Funds, REIT's, S&P 500 Index Fund, Rental Housing, Nasdaq 100 Index Fund, and the INdustry-specific Index Fund.

For a full explanation of all of these options, and tons of information about how to grow your money seeds, read my first book, "Passive Income: From Broke to 7 Figures in 12 Months."

This is a lot of information to process when you're considering where to plant your money-seeds so they grow into big money.

To make this a lot easier, and to get as much as you can out of your money, (not to mention - automating this process) it might benefit you to bring in the professionals. If you're feeling like this is not up your alley, but you like the idea of investing, It's time to hire a **financial planner.**

A financial planner is a highly trained professional that will help you manage your money and decide on investments. They can help you plant your money seed in the right soil. But, how can you find a planner that you trust and who can make your money grow.

Here are some tips for hiring a financial planner:

- Ask around! Chances are, someone you know, probably more than a few people you know, utilize a financial planner. The best tip is to get a list from the people you trust.
- Check credentials! You can do this on a web site called brokercheck.com. Adviserinfo.sec.gov is also a good option. These sites will give you the background and experience of the advisor and if there has ever been any disciplinary action taken against them.
- Know what you're looking for. Do you want a fiduciary or suitability standard advisor? A fiduciary advisor can only take a set fee to help you invest your money, and he or she is legally bound to act in your best interest, even above their own interest. A suitability standard advisor works on commission, and they're obligated to make suitable choices with your investments but could be swayed by their own interest. The positive is they take the risk with you.
- Shop around and ask questions. Ask them to describe their client experience. How do they communicate with

their clients and how often? How do they measure client success? Are they able to customize their approach to meet your needs? Make sure you feel comfortable with your chosen planner. They're going to be managing your future, and you need to feel good about that.

Hiring a good financial planner will help you increase your revenue without adding workload. Investments are a great form of passive income.

Local Guide Ad Sales Worksheet

To create your ad guide, and to figure out which businesses you can approach to purchase advertising, you'll need to brainstorm as many local businesses as you can think of. In this worksheet, you're going to do just that.

In the categies below list as many local businesses as you can think of.

Restaurant	Attraction	Gifts/Floral	Beauty	Bakery

CHAPTER FOURTEEN: RENT-TO-RICH SUCCESS STORIES!

So, now you've read all of the information and you know how it all works. In theory, you're convinced. But have people actually accomplished a six or seven figure income using Airbnb, Vrbo, and other vacation rental platforms? The answer is a resounding, "Yes!"

My rental company, Habytare, is just one example of this. Haytare has been bringing in a seven figure revenue since 2017, starting with rental properties in the Canary Islands and now renting beautiful holiday villas short term all over the world.

But I am not the only millionaire entrepreneur who has found success in this industry. Take a look at these real-life rent-to-rich stories.

> **SPOTLIGHT: AIRBNB MULTI MILLIONAIRES**
>
> The most successful Airbnb host of all time made $15.5 MILLION in one year renting out 881 properties across London, England.

You can bet he was not washing sheets and responding to guests. He implemented all of the autopilots so he could make millions of dollars - more money than some people see in a lifetime - in just one year.

The same holds true for the second most profitable Airbnb host - a superhost with 504 properties in Bali generating **$15.4 MILLION in revenue in one year.**

While these results are not typical, they are absolutely doable, and more and more Airbnb hosts are becoming millionaires in their first couple of years in the industry.

Jan Jens

Jan Jens created a rent-to-rent business with a net revenue of close to $8 million per annum, which he started with one luxury Miami rental property.

According to an interview with Jens in Forbes magazine, he arrived in the U.S. from Germany in his young twenties, not exactly sure how he was going to do it, but knowing he wanted to do it in the city his family vacationed in when he was a child- Miami.

With a small loan from his dad (which was repaid within three months), he rented his first luxury villa. His trick to creating one of the most sought-after properties in one of the hippest cities?

Customer service.

He was committed to making sure his customers could do whatever they wanted, whenever they wanted, when they were vacationing in his properties.

His reputation for top notch customer service quickly got around, and soon his villa was completely booked out. Jens was a millionaire within the first 18 months. But he didn't go hog-wild and spend his money like crazy. Instead, he strategically invested in more properties as well as advertising and automation optimization.

In 2018, he generated $7.5 MIL from 12 properties in Miami and was projected to make $10.5 MIL last year. Now, this thirty-year-old entrepreneur's company, Jatina Group, has a staff of six to handle most of the day-to-day business, but he takes care of his high-end and celebrity guests (of which there are many) personally.

Jens went from a $39,000 investment to $10.5 MILLION in revenue in six years. I'd say that's a rent-to-rich success story.

Evan K.

Evan's story doesn't reach as high as Jens', but his business is making him an incredibly comfortable living with plenty of free time for, well, actual living!

Evan is a young web developer who has now traveled to over seven countries and two continents in the last two years all while his Airbnb's are running on autopilot, earning him around $11,000 per month.

What would you do with an extra $11,000 per month?

Evan started out like many of the average Airbnb hosts. He was living in a $3100 one bedroom apartment in the Fisherman's Wharf area of San Francisco, and he was concerned about how he was going to pay rent if he had a slow month. (Those of us who run or have run our own businesses understand that feeling - it can feel like you're lugging around a suitcase full of rocks sometimes. It can be a constant underlying anxiety, unless you have secondary income streams.)

Evan's friend encouraged him to throw his living room up on AirBnB to help him make rent, and he did. He booked it the first night he had it listed, and got his first five-star rating.

In the next month, Evan **earned two times his rent** on just his living room rental. Of course, his apartment is in the heart of a very touristy area with hotel rooms going for $300-$500 per night, and as we know, location is key in real estate.

Evan had the location.

Evan has since expanded to renting three other properties in three different cities, and his businesses pretty much runs on autopilot.

FINANCIAL FREEDOM

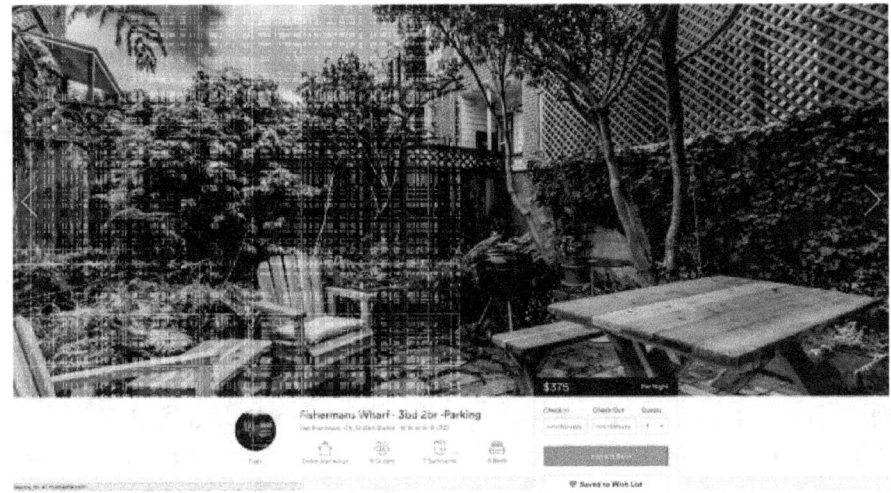

Now, with a six figure income flowing freely to him without much effort, he spends his time traveling the world, only coming back to home base when he wants to. He doesn't have to worry about his rent anymore, bringing in six figures per year working a few hours a week from wherever he is on the planet.

Evelyn B.

Evelyn Badia has made a career out of hosting since losing her job in the tv/commercial production business in 2010. With a six figure income from just two listings in Park Slope, Brookly, NY, Badia prides herself on the personal host experience and has since created another stream of passive income from her own branded hosting programs and books.

While Evelyn loves hosting and is very hands-on with that aspect of the business (she played to her strengths and what she loves), her method for building her business and becoming a top-rated host, booking out her property and giving a good guest experience, are the same techniques outlined in this book.

Evelyn has bYou can purchase Evelyn's host guides on her website, and see interviews with her on a number of websites highlighting the viability of a career in vacation rentals.

A six-figure income from doing what you love, and making a tidy passive income as an offshoot, Evelyn is truly an Airbnb success story.

P. Mccann

P. McCann was 52 when he spruced up his Sydney, Australia apartment to put up on Airbnb. He had traveled to New York and had such a positive experience staying at his first Airbnb there, spending half of what he would have for a hotel and extending his trip as a result, that it planted the seed for him to do the same with his own apartment back home.

McCann had his first guest booked within 24 hours, and was quickly booking out his place 28 or 29 days a month. He added a second apartment in the same building, and then a third location shortly after.

Now, McCann is making six figures and plans to **retire by the age of 57** on his rental income.

Aaron M.

Aaron is a former IT consultant who easily generates a six-figure income with just two Airbnb listings in Waikiki, Hawaii. Originally, Aaron and his wife listed the spare bedroom of their two-bedroom condo. This was in 2013. Soon after, they added a second condo and more than doubled their revenue.

Thne, in 2014, Aaron's IT contract ended and he and his wife decided to make Airbnb hosting their full time career. They rented a small apartment down the street from the two condos, stayed there themselves, and rented the full condos out on Airbnb (rather than just rooms in the condos).

That first year listing the two condos, the couples made

$124,000 and the next year it jumped to $138,000. And this is just from TWO PROPERTIES! Think about how much they could be making if they doubled their properties or more!

Ahmad And Christina

Ahmad and Christina are real estate investors who started their Airbnb business with three listings in the San Francisco area. And they really approached this as a business - a hospitality business, to be more precise.

Using all of the tips that we've gone over in this program, they were able to create beautiful listings for their nicely-furnished properties.

Their attention to detail and diligence paid off, and these two earn $7,000 - $10,000 per month just on these three properties.

And the crazy thing is, as full time real estate investors in their early thirties, this $100,000 per year income stream is just their side hustle!

While some vacation rental hosts are obviously managing huge rental property businesses raking in billions of dollars a year, others are happy and content making a "modest" $70,000 - $120,000 per year with the perks of a self-owned business: more freedom, upward mobility, shorter work days and weeks, and the list goes on.

The thing is that most of these people, and most hosts who put their properties on any one of these property management platforms, started out just like you! They were stuck in a job they didn't like, and they were ready and willing to make a change.

Now it's time for your homework... In the following worksheet, you're going to write your own success story! Why? Because whether you believe it or not, clearly visualizing your goal will help everything align for you to achieve it. So, get in there and really show yourself what you are aiming for.

My Success Story Worksheet (Example)

Visualization is an excellent exercise to help you keep your goals clearly in your sight. So, it's time for you to dig into your imagination. In the space below, I want you to write your own success story. BE AS DETAILED AS POSSIBLE.

(EXAMPLE) (written from the perspective of Corey B.)

Corey B. opened up her first Airbnb when she was twenty-seven. Having just moved to New York after taking a job with the NY Philharmonic, this midwestern girl quickly found herself flooded in bills- the heaviest being the rent on her two bedroom industrial apartment.

And guess what? Her roommate was getting married and moving out! Corey had to do something quick, but she didn't want to get a new roommate. Courntey fixed up the now-empty bedroom along with her own bedroom and listed the single room as one listing and the entire apartment as a second listing. (She'd stay with a friend if it booked out.)

In the first month, and after paying her rent and contributing to expenses at her friend's house, Courtney brought in a revenue of $4000 that first month. That was in 2020. Now, in 2025, Courtney has five listings on Airbnb, four in New York and one in Marbella, Spain, where Courntey spends much of her time in Spain's off-season. She has left her full time job and makes a quarter million dollars a year as a full time rent-to-rent vacation rental host, which she does while traveling the world and asking new friends in every country she can!

My Success Story Worksheet

Visualization is an excellent exercise to help you keep your goals clearly in your sight. So, it's time for you to dig into your imagination. In the space below, I want you to write your own success story. BE AS DETAILED AS POSSIBLE.

CHAPTER FIFTEEN: THE TAKEAWAY

How to be a Successful Rent to Rent Entrepreneur

Congratulations! You've made it to the end of *FINANCIAL FREEDOM : HOW TO MAKE 7 FIGURES PASSIVE INCOME WITH AIRBNB RENT TO RENT*. You're ready to become a short-stay rental host and the master of several tributaries to your passive income stream… and you're going to change your life forever.

No more nine to five. No more rush hour traffic. No more paycheck to paycheck. No more working hard and not getting anywhere. It's time for you to take control of your life and watch your revenue skyrocket!

I know that I have given you a lot of ideas, a lot of things to think about, a lot of actions to take… and I've told you about some phenomenal success stories of people who have been able to quit their day job and make more money working less from any place in the world (that has an internet connection).

But, now I have to tell you something you might be surprised to hear…. Although this is an "almost scientific" method based on statistical datas made by properties in the same neighborhood of yours and with the same specifications, and even by following step by step the indications I gave you in this book, it might not be as easy as pie. Execution always made a big part in successful business and also and especially your mindset and attitude.

What am I saying, now? I've just given you a whole program about how fantastic it's going to be to follow these simple steps to change your life. I've used words like simple, streamlined, and quick.

Now I'm saying it's not that easy? What could I possibly be doing to you, here? This is what I mean.

Have you ever heard the phrase, "The most successful people fail the most?"

So, what I'm telling you is, "Be prepared to fail, because you will, eventually." And that's to be expected, valued, and used to build your business up.

I'm here to tell you that in all of this, you're going to try some things that don't work. And that's completely okay. In fact, it is more than okay. It's exactly what you need to do.

Did you know that Steven Spielberg, whose cinematic output has reached over $9 billion, was rejected by the University of Southern California's School of Cinematic Arts… twice?!

He did not quit. And because he did not quit, the world has Star Wars!

Thomas Edison was told by his teachers that he was stupid. Over 1,000 patents later, he proved them wrong… and we have lights and motion pictures…

The key to success is to not give up.

In fact, the story of the biggest player in the short-stay rental game, a new kid on the block that changed the face of vacationing forever, Airbnb, has its own fail to succeed story.

The Airbnb Startup Story

The seed of Airbnb was planted several times without success before it finally took root. And when it did, it blossomed like nobody would have ever believed. I'd go so far as to say that Airbnb changed the vacation rental landscape like Apple changed personal communication.

But the story of this young company with a refreshing new concept is one not of a sudden miracle, but it's one of persistence, grit, overcoming fear and naysayers, and hustling until they won.

And they did it because no matter how hard they fell, they never lost faith in themselves and in their idea.

It's San Francisco, 2007. Two young guys, Brian Chesky and Joe Gebbia, had just traveled across the country from New York to move to the Bay Area. But the problem was that neither one of them had jobs, and they were struggling (as one would with no job- especially in San Francisco) to pay their rent.

So, what did they do? Did they pack it in and head back to New York? No, they did not.

With a little bit of creativity and a huge helping of "no fear," they saw a need and filled it. Quite literally. And they did it well enough to keep doing it over and over again.

They noticed that the hotels in the area were booked up solid with the influx of visitors to a local conference. So, they bought a couple of air beds, filled them with hot air, tossed them on the floor of their apartment and rented them out for $80 each per night - including breakfast!

The original name of Airbnb was literally AirBed & Breakfast. (As in, you get an airbed and some kind of food in the morning.

They gave their guests a (fairly) comfortable place to sleep and food in the morning, charging much less than the local hotels (not that you could get a room in one of the hotels, anyway, no matter how much you were willing to pay).

Their first guests were a 30-year-old man from India and a 35-year old Boston woman, plus a 45-year-old dad from Utah, all in for the conference. All sleeping in airbeds on Brian and Joe's floor, all trusting that the other people in the house were not murderers or rapists or weirdos. It took a lot of trust on everyone's part. But it worked!

Ta-dah! The first ever Airbnb guests were born.

It didn't take long before the duo, the pioneers of this new company, became three (no, they did not have a baby), and Harvard graduate Nathan Bleharcyk joined the team. But they were facing a problem-- they needed more users and more hosts if they wanted this to be a viable business model.

They figured, South by Southwest (SXSW) would be raking in the guests... but not so. They got two bookings during this hugely trafficked music festival.

But the team didn't give up. Instead, they rolled up their sleeves and got to work. They did some major website overhauling and relaunched in 2008 just prior to the Democratic National Convention in Denver which was set to draw over 20,000 people.

Every hotel in the Denver area was booked out. This was the perfect stage for the introduction of space-sharing rooms for let.

But the people were skeptical, even after more than 600 guests stayed at Airbnbs just during that convention.

The mindset was that "these are like-minded people hosting like-minded people." Obama supporters hosting other Obama supporters. The question on peoples' minds was, "What happens when this gets bigger, and it's not limited to a tiny demographic of decent people?"

People were making public comments about the whole business falling apart because nobody could trust that the hosts or the guests weren't going to be murderers, rapists, and thieves.

And at first, those naysayers were right. The launch success was short-lived. But once again, they pushed on and received their first funding in the form of $20,000 from Y Combinator, an incubator organization dedicated to funding promising startups.

They use this money to do some market research, and they hop on a plane to New York to meet the users in their largest market. And here's what they discover: Poor picture quality across the board is an impediment to booking out listings. So, they buy a good quality camera and photograph all the listings themselves, and they see an immediate boost in bookings.

(I can't stress enough - your photographs are key to your booking success!)

This brings us up to the start of 2009, and Y Combinator brings the team out to a three month training session... and the company is gaining momentum. Instead of just focusing on sharing rooms in one's own home, or mattresses on the floor, the company has shifted to every type of accommodation including whole homes or condos, cabins in the woods, Airstreams... you name it. By March, the new version of Airbnb has 2500 property listings and 10,000 registered users interested in renting a space in someone's home.

This moment marks a huge shift in the hotel and hospitality industry.

Airbnb currently boasts over 2 million listings in over 190 countries and 34,000 cities worldwide. Over 40 million guests have put their trust in the goodness of people (and the company - and its vetting system), and stayed in Airbnb properties.

This little company that started with three air mattresses and some cereal is now worth somewhere around $25.5 billion.

All because a couple of guys weren't afraid of some strangers on the floor, and never gave up on their incredible and crazy idea.

The moral of this story and the reason I'm telling it to you now is this.

You will stumble. You'll scrape your knees. But don't stay down. Instead, learn from the mistakes, tweak the program, make it better, and keep going. You have the spirit it takes to succeed!

If you do a Google search for "habits of successful people," you'll find a LOT of information. Some lists taut 50 habits, others say it's five. Still other sites or experts say it's personality traits, not habits, that help predict a person's capability for success.

But I believe that success is a combination of personality, drive, and habits. Here's a good start to how to be and stay successful in this rent-to-rent venture and in the rest of your life.

Daily Habits Of Successful People

Let's start with the microcosm and work our way up the to macrocosm. Meaning, let's take one day at a time and address simple daily habits that help cultivate (or are perhaps innate in) successful people.

1. **Get enough sleep.** Contrary to popular belief, the most successful people in the long run are not the ones who stay up all night- whether that be working or partying, pouring over spreadsheets or pacing their living room. Successful people prioritize sleep. Why? Because your body and your brain need sleep to function at their best. You can't be on point, solving problems, getting important work done, if you're trying to slide by on three hours. You need seven to nine hours of sleep per night to fully rejuvenate your body and refresh your brain. You'll stay physically healthier (lack of sleep leads to a broken down immune system) and mentally sharper, less irritable, and happier (yes, sleep makes you happier).

2. **Eat well, exercise, and drink water.** I know, these sound like tips from a health site, not a success plan. But it's true... successful people take care of their bodies by putting the right nourishment in and hydrating. You'd be surprised how much the rest of your life changes if you change one aspect of it. Change your body, change your business. Focus on eating plenty of fresh fruits and vegetables, lean proteins, and healthy fats. Drink water whenever you're thirsty, and remember to start your day with a glass - your body is most dehydrated when you first wake up. And exercise is important for a number of reasons, including that exercise releases endorphins in your brain that help relieve stress.

3. **Meditate or contemplate.** I'm not saying you have to choose a meditation practice, to sit cross-legged or chant (although you absolutely can do those things). But daily "time out" to sit quietly, contemplate, or let your mind just relax and be free, is a habit that most highly successful people have embraced. Meditation has been proven to reduce stress, and often when you clear your mind you make room for new and important thoughts and ideas.

4. **Express gratitude.** Whether this is through your mealtime prayer, a gratitude journal, or just by telling people you're grateful for their help, their input, their presence... The expression of gratitude on a regular basis seems to be a major theme across the span of successful individuals.

5. **Get organized.** This seems to be a tricky hone for a lot of people, but once you figure out a system to get and stay organized (in your office, online, in your home), everything will start to run like a well-oiled machine.

6. **Learn something every day.** In earlier chapters I talked about reading a book a week. This is along those same lines. Never get so full of yourself that you feel you have nothing else to learn. You always have something to learn, especially in this ever-changing world. You might read a book based on history, let your teenage nephew teach you how to operate a new app on your iPhone, or be open enough to learn something new about how to communicate with someone who is different than you. Life is all about learning, and when you embrace that, so many doors open for you.

Characteristics Of Successful People

I've already said that successful people are not afraid to fail. That's just one common characteristic among the most highly successful people. While I won't go so far to say that ALL successful people share these traits, there's enough of a common thread that they are worth mentioning for you to contemplate as you consider your journey and the process it is going to take to get you where you want to go.

- **Successful people step outside their comfort zone.** It takes a willingness to put the "known" aside to take a risk, start a new business, meet new people, make positive changes. Because most of us know, even positive changes can be scary. But you do not need to be afraid of the unknown. The only thing to be afraid of is stagnation. Don't ever let your fear, or your comfortable numbness, prevent you from living the life you've always wanted.

- **Successful people celebrate others' success.** The most successful people truly take joy in other peoples' success and happiness. They tend to draw people to them with this kind of enthusiasm and charisma, and they are often willing and eager to help others reach their goals. Truly successful people understand that there is room for everyone at the top.

- **Successful people love a challenge.** They do not shy away from problems, but they relish in tackling the issues head on. Perhaps this goes hand in hand with stepping outside of your comfort zone and not being afraid to fail. But successful people will be the first to dive into a challenge and offer creative ideas to solve problems.

- **Successful people have balance.** Most people cannot last long working nonstop… and over and over again it's proven that doing so does not get you further ahead. The most successful people are able to find a healthy balance between work and personal life. They do not put work over family or loved ones. They find time and space to relax, to have fun, and to connect with the people that are important to them. This includes balancing their business and their creative minds. Most successful people have hobbies and interests outside of their businesses, and that often includes creating - art, music, writing, et cetera.

- **Successful people have a clear mission.** Not only do they set goals for their business, and financial goals, but they have a clear mission in their lives. When your life has a mission, a purpose, beyond just making money, you are driven in ways you can't even start to imagine unless you have felt it. People with a clear mission can see their path laid out and they know how to get where they're going... and this process falls in line with all of their core beliefs, and they feel fulfilled.

Which of these characteristics do you already have? Which of these habits are already a part of your daily life? What things would you like to change and work on to help you have the habits and mindset of a highly successful person?

Use the worksheet at the end of this chapter to recall your strengths and pinpoint the areas you need to work on in order to be the most successful person you can be!

FINANCIAL FREEDOM : HOW TO MAKE 7 FIGURES PASSIVE INCOME WITH AIRBNB RENT TO RENT RECAP

In this program, you've learned how to create a motivated mindset, build the habits and characteristics of a successful person... and you were given the step-by-step, play-by-play process of how to build a seven-figure passive income using rental properties and home-sharing platforms.

You know why you want to get out of your nine-to-five, and you have the tools you need to stay motivated throughout the process of transitioning into your new business venture.

From this book you have learned:

- ★ THE INCREDIBLE BENEFITS OF CREATING A PASSIVE INCOME STREAM USING RENT-TO-RENT
- ★ HOW TO FIND & MAINTAIN YOUR MOTIVATION
- ★ THE DIFFERENCE BETWEEN SHORT-TERM RENTAL AND BEING A LANDLORD OR PROPERTY MANAGER
- ★ HOW TO FIND THE PERFECT PROPERTY
- ★ HOW TO WIN OVER YOUR LANDLORD
- ★ THE INS AND OUTS OF LEASES AND CONTRACTS

- ★ HOW TO GET STARTED LISTING YOUR RENTAL
- ★ HOW TO CHOOSE THE RIGHT PLATFORM/S FOR YOUR PROPERTY
- ★ HOW TO CHOOSE A CHANNEL MANAGER
- ★ THE BEST TIPS AND TRICKS TO MAXIMIZE OCCUPANCY & PROFIT
- ★ HOW TO WRITE THE OPTIMAL LISTING
- ★ EASY AUTOMATION FOR PASSIVE INCOME
- ★ HOW TO CREATE RELATED PASSIVE INCOME STREAMS
- ★ ABOUT SUCCESS STORIES FROM PEOPLE JUST LIKE YOU!

Now, it is my sincere hope that you take everything you've learned and put it into action! You have what it takes to have the life that you deserve!

FAB BALE

www.fabbaleinvest.com

fab@fabbaleinvest.com

www.ingramcontent.com/pod-product-compliance
Lightning Source LLC
Chambersburg PA
CBHW071349210526
45465CB00001B/29